Horses

The Ultimate Treasury

LONDON, NEW YORK,
MELBOURNE, MUNICH, AND DELHI

Project Editor Victoria Wiggins
Senior Art Editor Sheila Collins
Designers Jim Green, Katie Knutton,
Hoa Luc, Jeongeun Park, Mary Sandberg

Managing Editor Linda Esposito
Managing Art Editor Diane Peyton Jones
Category Publisher Laura Buller

Publishing Director Jonathan Metcalf
Associate Publishing Director Liz Wheeler
Art Director Phil Ormerod
Producer (Pre-Production) Adam Stoneham
Senior Production Controller Sophie Argyris
Picture Research Myriam Megharbi
Illustrator Dianne Breeze
Jacket Editor Manisha Majithia
Jacket Designers Nim Kook, Silke Springies

First American Edition, 2012

Published in the United States by
DK Publishing
375 Hudson Street
New York, New York 10014

Copyright © 2012 Dorling Kindersley Limited

2 4 6 8 10 9 7 5 3 1
001—186352—Oct/12

A catalog record for this book is available
from the Library of Congress.

ISBN: 978-0-7566-9801-0

Hi-res workflow proofed by Altaimage, UK
Printed and bound by Hung Hing, China

Discover more at
www.dk.com

Horses
The Ultimate Treasury

Written by
John Woodward

Consultant
Kim Bryan

Contents

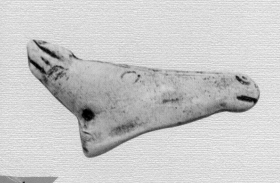

Early horses

Modern horses evolved on the grassy plains of North America more than four million years ago, eventually spreading into Asia across the dry land that once linked Alaska to eastern Siberia. For millennia they lived wild, but roughly 5,500 years ago the people of central Asia learned to tame them and, in time, how to ride them.

The horse family

Horses are part of a small family of animals consisting of eight closely related species of horses, asses, and zebras. They are the survivors of a much more diverse family that probably originated in North America about 50 million years ago. Their earliest ancestors were small, forest-living leaf-eaters, but over time the process of evolution gave rise to bigger animals specialized for life on the open grassy plains.

Beginnings

The earliest ancestor of modern horses was the size of a dog, and lived in woodlands and forests. Known to scientists as *Hyracotherium*, it had separate toes instead of single hooves, and its fossil remains show that it had low-crowned teeth suitable for eating the tender leaves of bushes rather than grass. Many more species of these browsing, forest-living horses evolved over time, together with others adapted to life on grasslands, but eventually all the browsing types died out.

The kiang (Equus kiang) is a wild ass that lives on the high-level grasslands of the Tibetan plateau.

Meet the family

The earliest horses belonging to the genus *Equus* seem to have evolved four to five million years ago in North America, and before long they spread to Eurasia. They gave rise to all the modern species of wild horses, asses, and zebras, as well as domestic horses and donkeys.

Bigger and faster

As time went on, the grassland horses evolved species with bigger teeth better suited to eating tough, fibrous grass. They also had longer legs with fewer toes, giving them the speed to escape predators. There were many types, but only the various *Equus* species have survived.

The donkey (Equus asinus) has been reshaped over time by selective breeding.

The domestic horse (Equus ferus caballus) is a race of the wild horse (Equus ferus).

Przewalski's Horse (Equus ferus przewalski) is the only surviving truly wild horse.

The Asiatic ass (Equus hemionus) still lives wild, but is now rare and endangered.

Plains zebras (Equus quagga) live in big herds on the African savannas.

Cave paintings

Horse's head carved from animal bone

Many Stone Age cave paintings in France and Spain show the wild horses that were roaming the plains of southern Europe around 18,000 years ago. This was roughly the height of the last ice age, when life was hard and people depended heavily on hunting wild animals—including wild horses—for food. They painted images of their quarry on the walls of caves, and miraculously some of these images have survived. The horses they depict are very similar to the most primitive wild horses still living today.

Horse painters

The painters were the Magdalenian people who lived from 18,000 to 10,000 BCE. The painted caves were possibly their sacred sites. In addition to painting, they made small carvings, including images of horses' heads.

Tough times

When the paintings were made, much of northern Europe was covered by ice. Farther south lay dry grassland inhabited by wolves, hyenas, bison, woolly mammoths, and reindeer like this one. Some animals and people would have migrated south to escape the harsh winters, returning in spring.

Horse's head carved from animal bone

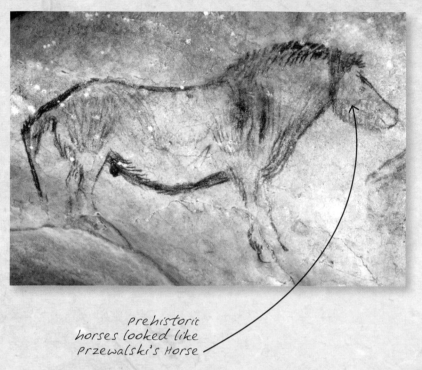

Familiar features

The horses in cave paintings, such as this one in the Niaux cave in southwest France, are heavily built, with a large, blocky head and an upright mane, much like Przewalski's Horse. Some paintings even show the same color pattern—dun, with darker legs. This doesn't mean that they were the same as Przewalski's Horse, but they were probably closely related.

Prehistoric horses looked like Przewalski's Horse

Hidden treasure

Unfortunately, when these caves are opened up, their paintings start fading away. So the finest images have now been reproduced for display in nearby replica caves like this one at Altamira in northern Spain, and the real caves are sealed up to preserve them.

Replica cave paintings in northern Spain

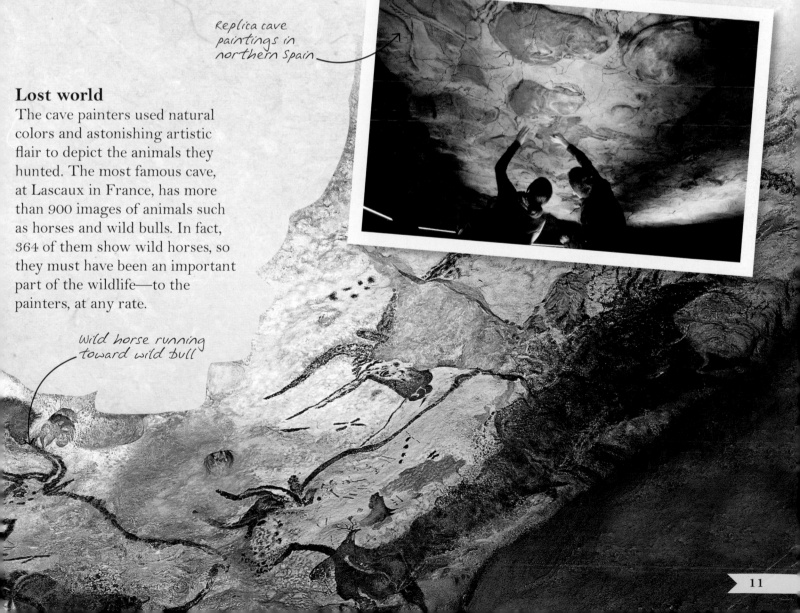

Lost world

The cave painters used natural colors and astonishing artistic flair to depict the animals they hunted. The most famous cave, at Lascaux in France, has more than 900 images of animals such as horses and wild bulls. In fact, 364 of them show wild horses, so they must have been an important part of the wildlife—to the painters, at any rate.

Wild horse running toward wild bull

Wild horses

Wild horses live in herds that roam the landscape in search of good grazing, sticking together for mutual defense against big predators such as wolves. This way of life is instinctive, for it has also been adopted by most domestic horses that have gone wild, such as Camargue horses, mustangs, and many native ponies. These feral horses live in much the same way as their distant ancestors of more than 5,000 years ago.

Grazing herds
Living in a herd with many eyes alert for danger is essential for any big prey animal that cannot hide from its enemies. Horses favor groups of up to 10 or so, but may briefly form bigger herds. Since their main food—grass—is very abundant, they can all feed together without competing for scarce resources.

Leading by experience
A typical herd includes a stallion, a small harem of mares, and their foals. Other herds consist solely of young males. A breeding herd is led by an experienced dominant mare who knows the best grazing sites and water sources. This black mare has led a group of mustangs to water while the bay stallion on the left tags along.

Fighting stallions

Mature stallions compete for control over mares. They may even fight by rearing up, biting, and kicking like these Camargue stallions. They also defend the herd from predators. On the African plains, for example, zebra stallions will lash out if a chasing hyena gets too close, and they can easily smash a jaw with a well-aimed kick.

Moving on

Stallions instinctively drive young males and females out of the herd, but young females from other herds often move in. If the lead stallion is injured or weakened he may be driven out by a healthier, younger horse—and because wild stallions lead a riskier life than mares, such takeovers are common.

Home on the range

Wild horses have home ranges that the stallion scent-marks with dung piles, especially during the breeding season. The herd wanders from place to place within this range depending on the seasons, weather, food, and water, so the horses know their territory—or at least the lead mare knows it.

The heavy head has small ears, a big jaw, and very large teeth

The neck is short and muscular, with a short, bristly, upright mane

The pale-colored muzzle is described as "mealy"

The legs are short and strong, with tough hooves

Przewalski's Horse

Identified in 1881 by Russian explorer Colonel Nicolai Przewalski, this rugged, big-headed animal is the only surviving purebred wild horse. Przewalski found it in western Mongolia, where it was on the edge of extinction because of hunting by the local people. Saved by captive breeding, it has been reintroduced to its native Asian steppes. Here it now lives in a fully wild state, but it is carefully protected as our last living link with the domestic horse's primitive ancestors.

Przewalski's Horse

Truly wild by nature, Przewalski's Horse is stubborn and often aggressive, making it almost impossible to domesticate.

Height 12–13 hands
Colors Dun; dark mane, tail, and legs

Tough survivors

These wild horses have been living wild on the grassy steppes of central Asia for at least 20,000 years, and probably for much longer. They are survivors from the last ice age, and they have inherited their ancestors' ability to thrive in a hostile climate by roaming widely over the plains in search of good grazing.

Similar breed

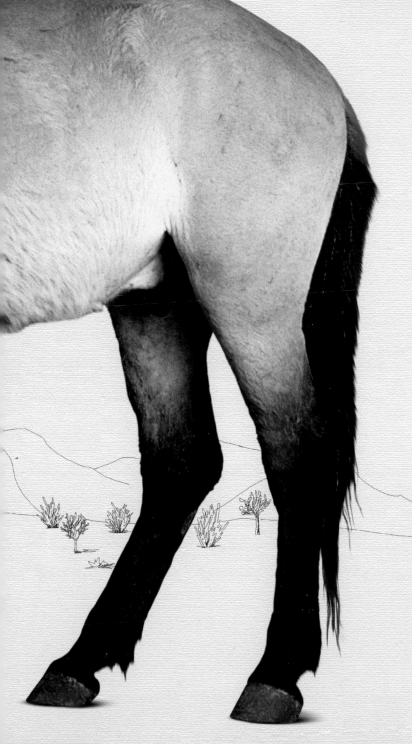

Tarpan

The original Tarpan was a wild ancestor of domestic horses. After extinction in 1887, it was artificially re-created by cross-breeding.

Height Average 13 hands
Colors Dun with dark dorsal stripe

Domestication

To the people who painted their images on the walls of caves, horses were just prey to be killed and eaten. Thousands of horse bones found in pits in Kazakhstan show that horses were still hunted 5,500 years ago. But these bones preserve evidence that some were used for other purposes, and within 1,500 years they were definitely being harnessed to chariots. By the late Bronze Age, warriors were riding their horses into battle.

Steppe horses
The first horses to be domesticated grazed the open grassy steppes of central Asia—ideal wild horse country. They were very similar to Przewalski's Horse, which has lived in this region for thousands of years, but it is more likely that they were the same wild race as the original Tarpan.

Earliest evidence
Some of the 5,500-year-old horse skulls found in Kazakhstan show "bit wear" on the teeth, indicating the use of bridles. The horses may have been mares tamed for their milk, which is a traditional drink in the region. But a few skulls with worn teeth were those of stallions, so it is possible that some animals were used as packhorses.

Chariot burials

By 2000 BCE, horses were being used to pull chariots. We know this because their bones have been discovered in graves alongside chariot wheels. The chariot burials also contained small studded cheekpieces made of deer antler, used with reins to guide the horses. This gold model chariot was made in Persia in the 5th century BCE.

Assyrian mounts

This stone relief from the 8th century BCE is one of many Assyrian carvings showing riders on horseback. They are the earliest solid proof of riding, which probably began about 200 years earlier. The rider has a saddle blanket but no stirrups, which were not invented until about 500 BCE.

Terror weapon

As soon as people learned to ride horses, they started riding them into battle. Some of the earliest mounted warriors were the Scythians of western Asia, who struck such terror into their victims that they were thought to be half-man, half-horse. This is the probable origin of the centaur legend.

The long neck is muscular and elegantly arched

The withers are well defined, and the shoulders are upright

The Sorraia has a heavy head with a slightly convex profile

Sorraia

Originating in the Sorraia river region of western Spain and Portugal, this very hardy pony has changed very little over the centuries and is probably a direct descendant of the ancestral Tarpan. It has several primitive features, and may have been one of the first domestic breeds. Easy to train, with a calm temperament, it was widely used for cattle ranching in the past. The Spanish took it to America, where its influence can still be seen in the half-wild mustangs.

The chest is deep but narrow

Back from the brink

In 1920, Sorraia ponies were living wild in Portugal, but in very small numbers. They were saved from extinction by zoologist Dr. Ruy d'Andrade, who kept a small herd living wild on his land. There are now more wild herds, but with only about 200 ponies in total, the breed is very rare.

Sorraia

The Sorraia looks very like the horses depicted in cave paintings dating from well over 10,000 years ago—another sign of its primitive nature.

Height 12–13 hands
Colors Dun or gray with dorsal stripe

Huçul

The Huçul is a primitive Polish breed from the Carpathian mountains. Small and robust, it makes an excellent pack pony.

Height 13 hands
Colors Mainly dun and bay

The legs are slender but strong

The hooves are tough

Konik

A Polish breed of ancient descent, the Konik is tough, willing, and usually docile. Semi-wild herds of Konik horses live in nature reserves across Europe.

Height 13 hands
Colours Dun with dorsal stripe

The story of Bucephalus

The legendary horse of Alexander the Great

Three centuries before the rise of the Roman Empire, Macedonia in Ancient Greece was ruled by a great king, Philip II, who loved to buy beautiful horses. One day, his 13-year-old son, Alexander, was with him when he went to view a magnificent black stallion with a white star on his brow. The animal had a wild temper, and whenever one of Philip's men tried to ride him he would buck and rear until the rider was thrown. The king was ready to send the horse away when Alexander asked if he could try to ride him. Philip refused, but Alexander persisted and finally his father gave in.

Alexander walked up to the nervous horse, took his bridle, and began patting him and talking to him quietly. As he led the horse around, he saw that the animal seemed frightened by his own shadow. Alexander turned him until he could no longer see it, then leaped on his back.

The stallion shied, but Alexander was able to keep his seat and calm him down. Within a few minutes, the horse relaxed, and Alexander was able to ride him before his father. Glowing with pride, Philip bought the stallion and gave him to Alexander, who named him Bucephalus.

In 336 BCE, Philip was killed, and Alexander became king of Macedonia at the age of just 20. He inherited a powerful army, including at least 5,000 cavalry, and within two years he invaded Asia and began to build a mighty empire covering much of western Asia and Egypt. The young horse-tamer had become Alexander the Great. But he took Bucephalus on all of his early campaigns, and at the Battle of Issus in 333 BCE the pair led a devastating cavalry charge against the army of the Persian king Darius III. They were inseparable.

Faithful steed

After Alexander's death, a legend grew up around Bucephalus, and other conquerers felt they needed favorite horses too. They included Napoleon, who, from 1800 to 1815, rode into battle on a gray Arab stallion named Marengo.

Exotic breed

No one knows exactly which part of the ancient world Bucephalus came from. He may have been bred in nearby Thessaly, but it is more likely that he was a Turkoman stallion, similar to the Akhal-Teke horse that has been bred for centuries in Turkmenistan.

Seven years later, Alexander was fighting a battle by the Jhelum river in what is now northern Pakistan. The fighting was fierce, and Bucephalus was in the thick of it. Alexander won the battle, but lost his beloved horse, who died soon afterward. A grieving Alexander founded a city in his honor near the battlefield, naming it Bucephala. The city vanished long ago, but one day it may be rediscovered—along with the tomb of the black stallion who carried his master to victory and glory.

This ancient sculpture shows Bucephalus at the Battle of Issus

The Camargue has a heavy head with short ears

The neck is strong but unusually short

The body is deep in the girth

Camargue

Ponies have lived wild on the Camargue—the swampy, salty Rhône delta of southern France— for thousands of years. They are of ancient descent, with some Arab and Barb blood, and their harsh existence has made them very hardy and strong. They breed at will, but low-grade stallions are gelded during regular roundups. Some Camargues are also trained for riding, and are the traditional mount of the Camargue cowboy (*gardian*) for herding the local black cattle.

Nomadic herds

Wild Camargues live in herds like their ancestors, roaming over the coastal marshes where they feed on rough grass and reeds. Centuries of surviving on such poor fare have made them resourceful and tough, and although they are slow to mature, they are very long-lived.

Camargue

Powerful, agile, and sure-footed, with quiet temperaments, Camargues are now widely used for trekking over their native delta.

Height 13.1–14.1 hands
Colors Gray

The back is short and strong, with a low-set tail

Camargue brand mark

The legs are strong and well shaped, with very hard hooves

Mustang

In North America, feral horses—domestic horses run wild—are called mustangs. Originally Spanish in type, they are very variable.

Height 13.2–15 hands
Colors Any color

Brumby

Australian feral horses are descended from a broad range of breeds. They are extremely hardy, willful, and difficult to tame.

Height Up to 15 hands
Colors Any color

Horses
that made an
empire

Rising from obscurity to rule over half the world, Ghengis Khan was an aggressive empire-builder who conquered most of central Asia in the early 13th century. He achieved this by uniting the nomadic Mongol tribes under his command, and exploiting their superb horsemanship to create a force of high-speed hit-and-run raiders. Their organization and discipline were astounding, making them the most feared and effective cavalry in history. But they carried out their conquests with appalling cruelty, destroying entire cities.

Great Khan
Born in Mongolia around 1160, the man who became Ghengis Khan was one of seven children. He married young, but his wife was kidnapped by a rival tribe. After forming an alliance with two other tribes to get her back, he made more alliances that led to his being proclaimed Khan (emperor). Soon after this, he began the invasions that built his empire.

Mongol horsemen

The Mongol tribes had a long tradition of horsemanship that still survives on the steppes of Mongolia. Their skill was essential for herding horses and other livestock, but it was refined by tribal wars. The tribesmen learned how to fight on horseback and make long journeys—abilities that were vital to Genghis Khan's strategy.

Fearsome riders

The Mongols fought on horseback, mounted on their tough steppe ponies. They had stirrups, which allowed them to turn and shoot in any direction. Each warrior had three or four mounts, swapping between them to travel at high speeds for hours on end. They would cover up to 100 miles (160 km) a day to take their enemies by surprise and destroy them.

The Mongols traveled long distances to reach their targets, and attacked at high speed

War game

Unlike most of their opponents, the Mongol warriors trained constantly to perfect their horsemanship. This may have inspired the ferociously violent team game of buzkashi, still played on the central Asian steppes. The idea is to grab the headless carcass of a calf or goat from the ground while riding at full gallop, get it clear of the other players, and use it to score a goal.

Arab

The head is short, with a dished (inward-curving) profile and wide forehead

The most famous of all breeds, the Arab is also one of the oldest. Archaeological evidence suggests that it is at least 4,500 years old, and stemmed from a wild horse quite unlike those of the northern steppes—possibly the Caspian. Since records began, the breed has stayed pure, preserving its distinctive dished face, arched neck, high-set tail, and proud, prancing action. It is the ultimate hotblood (see page 31), used to improve and create other breeds such as the Thoroughbred.

The long neck is arched and very mobile

Similar breeds

Barb

The North African equivalent of the Arab, the Barb has an equally ancient history. It is less graceful, but tough and very fast.

Height 14–15 hands
Colors Gray, bay, black, and chestnut

Tersk

This new breed was developed in southwest Russia by crossing Arabs with local horses. The result is both robust and elegant.

Height 14.3–15.1 hands
Colors Mainly gray; also chestnut

Desert horse

As its name suggests, the Arab probably originated in the Middle East, in the region between Arabia and Turkey. The earliest known breeders were the Bedouin desert tribes, who, unusually, valued Arab mares more than stallions, because they were calmer in battle. Today, there are Arab breeders worldwide.

The shoulders are long and sloping, and the withers not too prominent

The chest is deep and broad

Arab

Elegant and fast, with a light, graceful, almost floating gait, the Arab also has terrific stamina and durability.

Height 14.1–15 hands
Colors Mainly bay, gray, and chestnut

Native ponies

Ponies have been living wild in many parts of the world for centuries, and some may be the direct descendants of the wild horses of prehistory. Hard living has made them tough, self-reliant, and sure-footed—and when tamed they are docile, adaptable, and surprisingly strong.

Breeds and types

All horse breeds have been created by people, by selecting breeding animals for characteristics such as strength, speed, toughness, endurance, size, or color. Over time, these characteristics have been exaggerated and refined, and because there is no ideal combination, each breed has its own unique character and appearance. However, every breed is part of a broader category known as a type, which describes its main function.

Raw material
The first domestic horses were bred from wild "steppe horses" like Przewalski's Horse. But the diversity of modern breeds suggests that some were at least partly bred from other wild races. Recent advances in the analysis of DNA may reveal the truth.

Selective breeding
Wild stallions compete to mate with mares, so the strongest stallions father most of the young and pass on their strong genes. One of the main aims of breeding is to refine this process by selecting which stallion mates with which mare. With luck, the resulting foal will combine the most desirable traits of both parents.

Breed societies
The characteristics of each breed are tightly defined by its breed society, which controls breeding by registering approved stallions and mares in a studbook. Depending on breed, a qualifying horse must be either purebred or meet a strict standard laid down by the society.

Coldblood

Warmblood

Hotblood

Amazing diversity

Local horse breeders have created
more than 300 breeds, including
this big black Friesian stallion and
his diminutive Shetland companion.
Each breed has its unique strengths,
and while most of them have
stayed local, some are now
bred all over the world.

Types

Any horse is also a "type." This
describes its main use, size, and
shape. Types include hack, hunter,
riding pony, heavy draft, and
light draft. A horse's type also
indicates its temperament:
Coldbloods are placid workers
while hotbloods are flighty racers,
and well-bred warmbloods
combine the best of both.

Broad forehead, with hooded, wide-set eyes

powerful, weight-bearing shoulders and thick, warm mane

Mealy color on muzzle

Exmoor

This very hardy pony is the oldest and purest of Britain's native breeds. The pale "mealy" color around its eyes and on its muzzle and underbelly are a primitive feature, probably inherited from ancient wild horses. Despite its small size, it is very strong, with great stamina, and its innate intelligence makes it ideal for riding on the rough terrain of its native moorland in southwest England. It can be headstrong, but well-trained Exmoors make good children's ponies, and they work well in harness.

Moorland home
Ponies have roamed Exmoor since before the last ice age, although such herds are now rare. Their hooded "toad" eyes and double-layered waterproof winter coat protect them from the unpredictable moorland weather. Semi-wild Exmoor ponies are naturally wary of humans.

Exmoor

The Exmoor breed has changed little since the Iron Age, when the ponies were used to pull chariots.

Height 12–12.3 hands
Colors Bay, brown, or dun

Compact, muscular body, with a deep chest and a level back

Mealy color on underbelly

Short legs with black markings and hard, neat feet

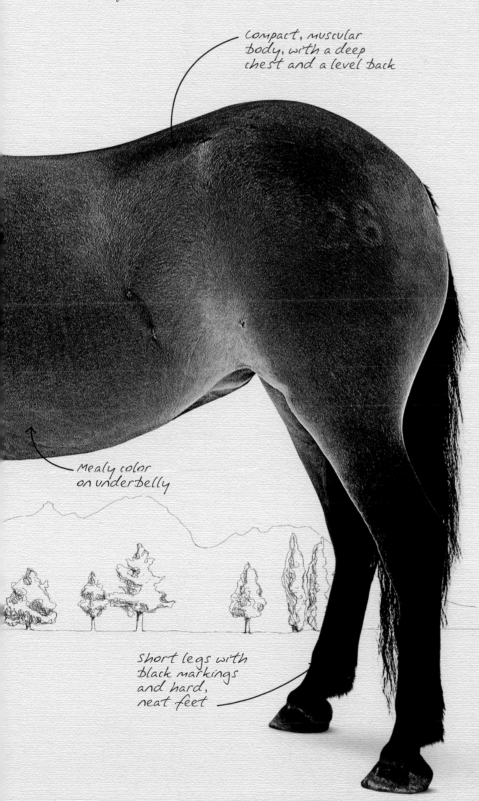

Similar breeds

Dartmoor

Also from the moors of southwest England, this is an excellent riding pony, with good conformation and a sweet temper.

Height 11.1–12.2 hands
Colors Mainly bay, brown, or black

Dales

The Dales was originally bred for use as a strong, hardy pack pony in the north of England, but is now used for riding and farm work.

Height 13.2–14.2 hands
Colors Mainly black, brown, or bay

New Forest

This tough, yet docile pony is derived from the ponies that lived half-wild in southern England, but is influenced by other breeds.

Height 12–14.2 hands
Colors Any solid color

Mythical horses

For centuries horses were seen as emblems of power and conquest, so it is not surprising that myths and legends grew up around them. At their simplest, these legendary horses were no more than wonderfully strong, fit, intelligent, and beautiful. But over time, they acquired fabulous attributes such as wings, horns, and even multiple heads and legs. Most of these mythical horses had supernatural powers that enabled them to whisk their riders through space and time—but some mythical horses were agents of death and destruction.

Spiral horn was thought to have magical properties

The unicorn
The mythical unicorn of medieval Europe was usually depicted as a pure white horse with a single spiral horn. It was a symbol of purity, and its horn was believed to have magical properties. This belief inspired a lucrative trade in the spiral tusks of Arctic narwhals, which people naturally assumed were the horns of unicorns.

White charger
The beautiful, perfect horse of legend was nearly always white—for example, the white horse of St. George, and Kanthaka, the white horse that was said to be the favorite of Prince Siddhartha, who became the Buddha. This tradition may have inspired one of the earliest horse images that isn't part of a cave painting—the colossal Bronze Age white horse carved on a hill at Uffington in southern England.

Magic powers

Some of the more fantastic mythical horses have extra legs or heads. In Ancient Norse mythology, the god Odin rode the eight-legged horse Sleipnir, which bore his rider to heaven and the land of the dead. Hindu mythology features the magical seven-headed flying horse Uchchaihshravas, the king of horses born from the churning of the cosmic ocean.

stars represent the constellation Pegasus

Winged Pegasus

Many mythical horses were embellished with wings. The most famous is Pegasus, the winged horse of Greek mythology, who was captured by the hero Bellerophon and ridden to defeat a monster called the Chimera. His form is outlined by a star constellation, as shown in this 15th-century image. A similar winged horse called Tianmar appears in Chinese folklore, and in Islamic tradition the archangel Gabriel has a winged horse called Haizum.

Devil horse

Some mythical horses had deadly powers. They include Celtic water horses like the Kelpie, which carried their victims underwater to drown. This Hindu image shows the horse-demon Keshi, sent to destroy the god Krishna, who killed the horse by thrusting his arm into its mouth to suffocate it.

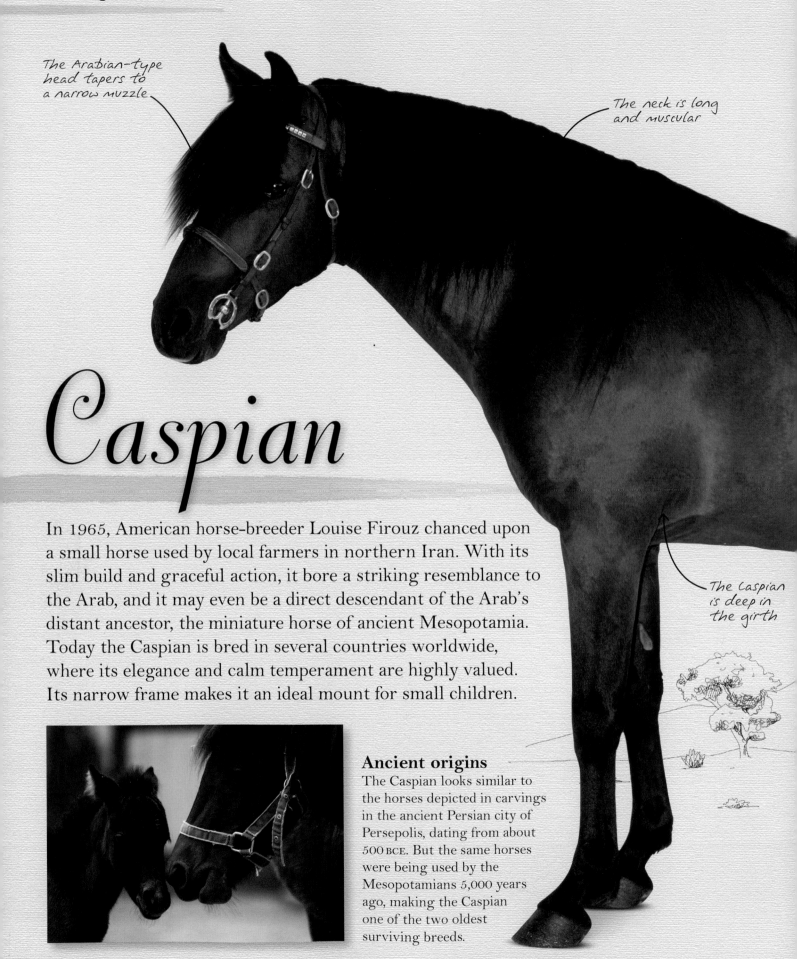

The Arabian-type head tapers to a narrow muzzle

The neck is long and muscular

Caspian

The Caspian is deep in the girth

In 1965, American horse-breeder Louise Firouz chanced upon a small horse used by local farmers in northern Iran. With its slim build and graceful action, it bore a striking resemblance to the Arab, and it may even be a direct descendant of the Arab's distant ancestor, the miniature horse of ancient Mesopotamia. Today the Caspian is bred in several countries worldwide, where its elegance and calm temperament are highly valued. Its narrow frame makes it an ideal mount for small children.

Ancient origins
The Caspian looks similar to the horses depicted in carvings in the ancient Persian city of Persepolis, dating from about 500 BCE. But the same horses were being used by the Mesopotamians 5,000 years ago, making the Caspian one of the two oldest surviving breeds.

Caspian

Used in harness for centuries, the Caspian has a natural grace and agility that make it excellent for riding, especially by children.

Height 10–12 hands
Colors Bay, gray, and chestnut

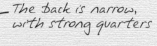

The back is narrow, with strong quarters

Mongolian

This is another ancient type, derived from the wild horses of the Asian steppes. It is very hardy, and has amazing endurance.

Height 12.2–14.2 hands
Colors Mainly dun, bay, and black

The legs are strong and fine, with extremely tough hooves

Batak

Part-Mongolian and part-Arab, the Batak is an Indonesian breed, locally popular as a riding pony and for light harness work.

Height Up to 13 hands
Colors Any color

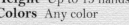

Horse sense

Horses are naturally sociable herd animals, so they need to communicate with others constantly. This has refined both their intelligence and their senses, making them acutely aware of one another. Their wild ancestors also had to be constantly alert to danger from predators such as wolves, so domestic horses have inherited a keen awareness of their surroundings, noticing every change and flicker of movement. Nothing escapes them.

All-around vision

A horse has big eyes set high on the side of its head for all-around vision. Its long muzzle allows it to watch for danger while it is grazing in long grass. It has roughly 65 degrees of binocular vision, which is vital for judging distance, and better night vision than us, but its color vision is poor—it cannot see red.

Social scents

Like most social mammals, horses have a highly developed sense of smell for identifying friends and strangers. They can enhance it by using the lip-curling flehmen response— sometimes called the "horse laugh"—to force air into a special sense organ at the bottom of the nasal cavity.

Acute hearing

A horse has very sensitive ears, and by moving them it can focus on a sound source and locate it without moving its head. This ear movement betrays what a horse is thinking—when the ears are pricked forward, for example, it is listening hard. Other horses are aware of this, so it is an important part of social communication.

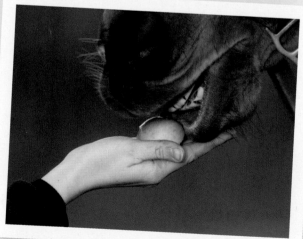

Good taste

Although not as important as some of its other senses, a horse's sense of taste helps it pick and choose when it is grazing, enabling it to reject the bitter tang of something that might be poisonous. But it works the other way too, because horses clearly enjoy eating sweet treats like this juicy apple.

Touch sensitive

Horses have a well-developed sense of touch. If you watch a horse in its paddock in summer, you will often see it twitch its flank muscles to shrug off a fly. This isn't just irritation—some flies are bloodsuckers or parasites. Horses often stand together, head to tail, and use their tails to help keep such flies at bay.

The neck is elegant and well arched

The head is well balanced, with large, gentle eyes

Well-conformed shoulders allow a good length of stride

Connemara

Named after the rainswept, mountainous region of western Ireland where it has lived wild for centuries, the Connemara is a rugged native pony with an infusion of Welsh, Arabian, and Asian blood. The combination has resulted in a tough, intelligent breed with a touch of class that allows it to compete regularly in show jumping and even dressage events. It is now popular all over the world, both as a riding pony and for driving in harness.

The chest is deep and broad

Reliable ride
Although more elegant than most native ponies, the Connemara still has all the ruggedness and common sense that enabled it to eke out a living on the boggy mountain slopes of its native land. This makes it a very dependable, sure-footed mount for riding over rough country.

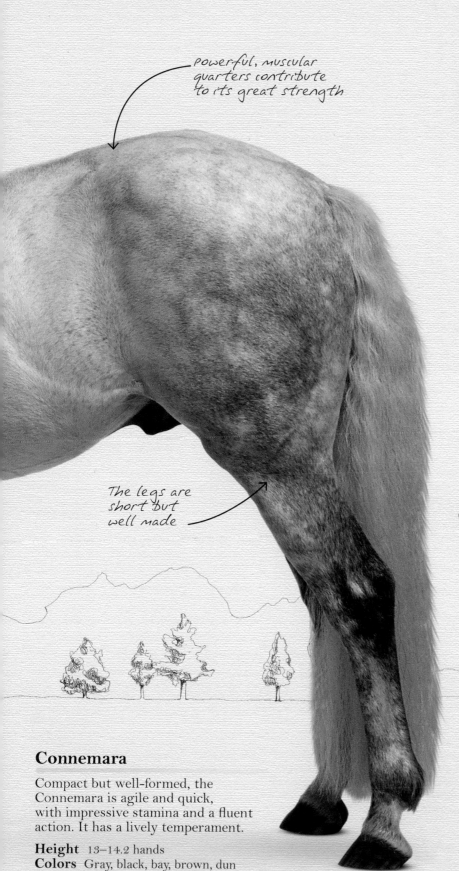

powerful, muscular quarters contribute to its great strength

The legs are short but well made

Welsh Mountain Pony

The oldest, smallest, and most elegant of the four types of Welsh ponies, this resilient, athletic breed is ideal for young riders.

Height Up to 12.2 hands
Colors Any solid color

Connemara

Compact but well-formed, the Connemara is agile and quick, with impressive stamina and a fluent action. It has a lively temperament.

Height 13–14.2 hands
Colors Gray, black, bay, brown, dun

Welsh Pony

One of four Welsh breeds, which also include the two Cob types, the Welsh Pony has some Arab and Barb blood and is a handsome riding pony.

Height Up to 13.2 hands
Colors Any solid color

Gypsy horses

Most vardos are painted in rich colors, with ornate decorations

For hundreds of years, Gypsies traveled the roads of Europe in often beautifully carved and decorated horse-drawn living wagons known as vardos. They also used small two-wheeled carts drawn by light ponies. These horses and ponies were essential to their way of life, and although modern Gypsies prefer motor vehicles, breeding and trading horses is still a vital part of the Gypsy tradition. However, their ideal horse does not conform to any of the more familiar breeds, so over the years Gypsy breeders have created their own.

On the road
Many types of horses were used to haul the vardos, but the Romany Gypsies of Britain and Ireland created a distinctive breed with enough strength and endurance to pull a heavy wagon all day, a calm temperament, and the ability to subsist on whatever grazing it could find on the roadside. Known as the Gypsy Cob, it is often piebald, with a luxuriant mane and tail, and well-feathered feet.

Racing ponies
Lighter ponies are often harnessed to two-wheeled barrows, or the lightweight sulkies used for trotting races. Here, a pony is put through its paces along a public road known as "Flashing Lane" at the Appleby Horse Fair in northern England.

Decorative feature with gold detail

This Gypsy Cob is pulling the vardo, while the other horse walks alongside

Breed status

Although the Gypsy Cob was originally just a type of horse bred for a practical purpose, it has recently become a recognized breed. Also called the Gypsy Vanner, it can be any color—although piebald or skewbald are preferred. It is popular in the United States, where there are different size classes for "mini Gypsies," "classic Gypsies," and "grand Gypsies."

Appleby Fair

Each spring, the town of Appleby-in-Westmorland in Cumbria, northern England, hosts the Appleby Horse Fair. Devoted to Gypsy horse trading and related activities, it has existed since at least 1685 and is the largest fair of its kind in the world. During the weeklong event, there are horses everywhere—even in the river, where they are washed.

Short but sturdy

Shetlands are remarkably strong for their size, and on their native islands they were used to haul heavy peat and seaweed, both as pack ponies and harnessed to carts. The breed is very hardy, with a thick winter coat to keep out the cold, and a luxuriant mane and tail.

The shoulders are sloping, with well-defined withers

The neck is strong and slightly crested

Shetland

Famous as the smallest British native pony, this resilient breed developed in the Shetland Islands off northern Scotland. Its ancestors may have reached Shetland during the last ice age, when the islands were linked to the mainland because of low sea levels. They were isolated there until the 19th century, when their small size led to many being used in coal mines as pit ponies. Today, they are used as children's ponies, or just treated as pets.

A Shetland has a deep, thickset body

The feet are strong and rounded

Shetland

The first recorded sighting of small ponies with great strength on Shetland dates from 1730, but the breed's studbook was not created until 1890.

Height Up to 10.2 hands
Colors Mainly black, but very varied

The back and loins are short, with strong quarters

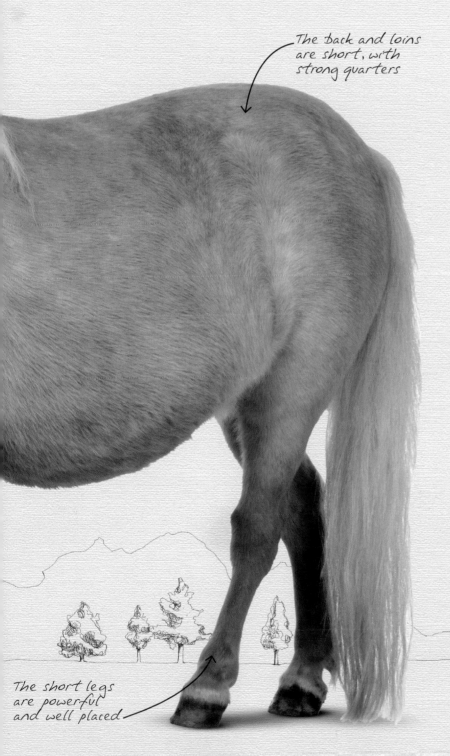

The short legs are powerful and well placed

Similar breeds

Highland

Used for centuries in Scotland for every purpose, the versatile Highland is a tough native type with Asian and Arab blood.

Height 13–14.2 hands
Colors Dun, gray, bay, and black

American Shetland

Crossing Shetlands with Hackney Ponies, Arabs, and others created this far more refined breed, often used in harness.

Height Up to 11.2 hands
Colors Any solid color

Australian Pony

This elegant pony is a recent creation, from many breeds including Welsh Mountain. It is a gentle children's pony.

Height 12–14 hands
Colors Any solid color

Understanding horses

A wild horse's survival depends on being part of the herd, and domestic horses have inherited this strong social instinct. They have also retained a snap response to possible danger that serves them well in the wild, but can make them behave very nervously in unfamiliar situations. However, horses learn fast and they have good memories, enabling them to master precise movements and perform complex routines.

Basic instinct
A wild horse relies on its sharp senses and speed to escape predators, so it is naturally fearful and flighty. A domestic horse is the same—it is always on the alert for danger, and may even sleep standing up. Its instinct when faced with any kind of threat is to bolt.

Happy stallions
Stallions can be aggressive toward each other, especially in the company of mares. But they are usually fine at other times. Young wild stallions live in bachelor herds, and this group of young Connemara stallions is clearly getting along well. A lot depends on good training.

Bad habits
Unfortunately, a horse can develop bad habits as well as good ones. They include stable vices such as crib biting, in which a horse seizes a rail in its teeth and pulls at it while sucking in air. Such vices may be caused by boredom, lack of exercise, or isolation from other animals.

Learning curve
This grey Lusitano stallion is performing the Spanish walk, lifting each foreleg high off the ground. Horses learn such skills quite readily, and as many riders know, they also have excellent memories for places and well-trodden routes.

Good companions

Horses are herd animals with a strong social instinct. They need company—ideally other horses that they can bond with, so they can all enjoy the benefits of mutual grooming. But a horse can also form a bond with other animals, such as goats, donkeys, or even sheep.

The story of Chetak

The horse who gave his life to save his master

The battle had reached a turning point. The air was filled with the deafening roar of war—the snorting of horses, the stamping of elephants, the whistle of spears hurtling through the air, and the agonized cries of dying men. The ground was ankle-deep in mud and blood, and discarded weapons lay trampled underfoot.

Chetak's elephant-trunk disguise

The year was 1576, and in northwest India the heavily outnumbered Rajputs were fighting for their lives in the Battle of Haldighati against the forces of the Mughal Emperor Akbar. They had almost lost hope when into the fray galloped their leader, Maharana Pratap, riding his warhorse Chetak—a beautiful Marwari with a blue tinge to his glossy white coat. But Chetak's elegant face was hidden by a mask with a long trunk, making him look like a baby elephant.

Chetak charged through the enemy ranks until he reached the enemy general Man Singh, who was riding majestically on an enormous elephant. Confused by Chetak's disguise, the elephant hesitated, and at a roar from Pratap, Chetak threw back his head and reared up, placing his front hooves on the elephant's head. Pratap hurled his spear, but Man Singh ducked and the spear struck his elephant rider instead.

With his rider dead, the elephant panicked and tried to escape. Like the other war elephants, he had a sword tied to the tip of his trunk, and as he swung around, the sword slashed one of Chetak's legs. With a squeal of agony, Chetak lurched back and galloped off the battlefield.

Chetak's wound was deep, but he ran on, carrying his master safely away from the battle. Eventually, weakened by loss of blood, but knowing that his rider would be safe, he collapsed by a stream and died. Today, a monument stands by the stream in this now peaceful place, ensuring that the memory of Chetak's sacrifice lives on.

Brave Chetak died knowing he had saved his master

Elephant mask

The Rajputs often disguised their Marwari horses with trunks like this, because the elephants of the enemy would not attack what seemed to be their own young. They also trained their horses to rear up high enough to reach the elephant riders.

Marwari horse

The Rajputs created the Marwari horse—bred and trained to be hardy, intelligent, and amazingly brave in battle. Its distinctive curved, mobile ears, like those of the Kathiawari breed, give it very acute hearing and a swift response to danger.

Haflinger

The head is small and
elegant, with big eyes
and small ears

The neck is
strong, and
always has a
flaxen mane

The Haflinger
has wide nostrils

Originating in the mountainous region around the
village of Hafling in the Austrian Tyrol, this ancient
breed seems to have stemmed from a cross between
Arabs and local mountain ponies. More Arab blood
was introduced in the 19th century to create a pony
that combines elegance with sure-footed strength and
durability. Since then, it has been purebred to the point
where there is very little variation, and it nearly always
has the same distinctive colors.

The chest
is deep

Mountain breed
The tough constitution of
the Haflinger makes it an
ideal pony for working in
harness in the demanding
climate and terrain of the
mountains. But it also makes
an excellent mount, with
a calm, docile nature
that is ideal for young,
inexperienced riders.

Haflinger

Four of the five main Haflinger bloodlines can be traced back to one 19th-century Arab stallion called El Bedavi XXII.

Height 13.1–14.2 hands
Colors Chestnut; flaxen mane and tail

The back is long and muscular

The legs are short but strong

The feet are clean, with very little feather

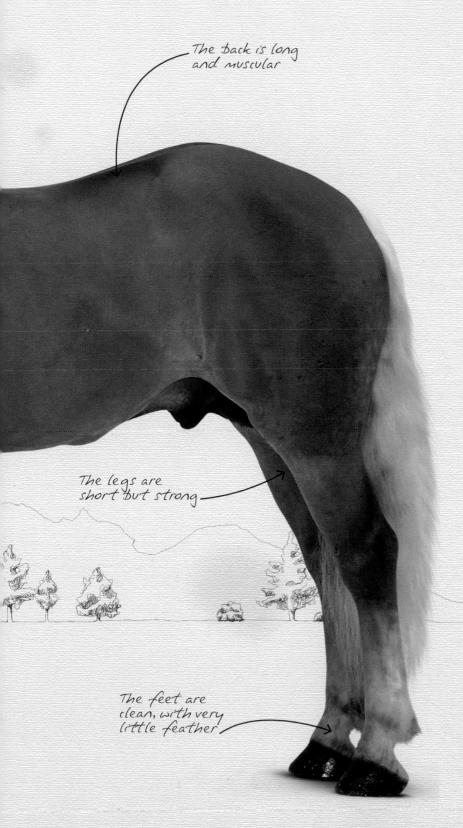

Avelignese

Closely related to the Haflinger, and very similar in appearance, this Italian breed is strong, versatile, and very sure-footed.

Height Up to 14.3 hands
Colors Chestnut; flaxen mane and tail

Pindos

Developed in the dry, demanding climate of central Greece, this mountain pony is exceptionally hardy and can survive on very little food.

Height Up to 13 hands
Colors Bay, black, brown, or dark gray

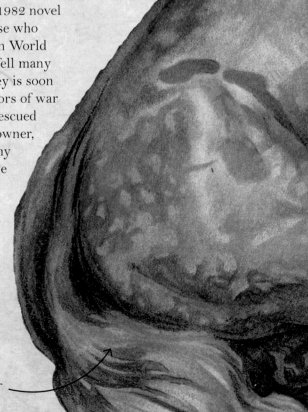

Horse heroes of fiction

Black Beauty
In Anna Sewell's "autobiography of a horse," Black Beauty describes the joys and hardships of his life and those of other horses in Victorian England. One aim of the novel was to promote animal rights by exposing the cruel treatment routinely endured by many horses. This is the cover of the first edition.

Many books feature horses. Most of these fictional animals are just accessories to the human action, although some are the main characters' trusted companions. In a few stories, however, horses are the principle characters—heroes in their own right, with their own voices. This tradition goes back a long way, but the first serious attempt to depict a horse's point of view was the novel *Black Beauty*, written in 1877. Since then, horses have figured prominently in many novels, and some of these have been made into very successful plays and movies.

War Horse
Michael Morpurgo's 1982 novel centers on Joey, a horse who is shipped to France in World War I—a fate that befell many horses at the time. Joey is soon caught up in the horrors of war on both sides, but is rescued by his young former owner, who enlists in the army to find him. This scene shows one of the astonishing puppet horses used in a stage play of the story.

A Houyhnhnm talks to Gulliver

National Velvet

Published in 1935, *National Velvet* by Enid Bagnold tells the story of a horse called The Pie, won in a raffle by 14-year-old Velvet Brown. She trains him up to win the British Grand National, with her as jockey. The 1944 film of the book made a star of the 12-year-old Elizabeth Taylor.

The Black Stallion

This scene from a 1979 film shows the opening episode of a series of children's books written by Walter Farley between 1941 and 1989. The stallion survives a shipwreck on a desert island along with teenager Alec Ramsay. The pair become lifelong companions, and are involved in many exciting horse-related adventures.

Gulliver's Travels

In 1726, Jonathan Swift published his satirical novel *Gulliver's Travels*. Near the end of the book, Gulliver meets a race of highly intelligent horses called the Houyhnhnms, who live alongside the savage but near-human Yahoos. The Houyhnhnms are civilized and rational, but the Yahoos are brutal and stupid. On his return, Gulliver realizes that he prefers the company of horses, and spends most of his time in the stables.

Fjord Pony

With its dun coat, dark dorsal stripe, and thick, bristly, two-tone mane, the Fjord Pony is clearly a very primitive breed, closely allied to the primeval horse of the Asian steppes. It has been domesticated for centuries in Norway, and was the horse used by the Vikings for both riding and draft work—it was probably the first horse to be used for plowing. It is tireless and very strong, and despite its wild appearance, it has a docile nature.

The upright mane has a dark central stripe, emphasized by clipping

Similar breeds

Icelandic Horse

A mixture of Fjord and Celtic blood, the Icelandic Horse is well known for its running walk and homing instinct.

Height 12–14 hands
Colors Any color

Gotland Pony

An ancient breed from the Swedish island of Gotland, this hardy pony is a fast trotter, often used in races.

Height 11–13 hands
Colors Any solid color

Tough but willing

Having survived and bred in the wintry Norwegian climate for at least 1,000 years, the Fjord Pony is very hardy. It is used as an all-around work and riding pony throughout Scandinavia, and its qualities of strength and willingness have made it popular in many other regions worldwide.

The legs are short and sturdy

The feet are very hard

Fjord Pony

These ponies breed very true to type, showing that they have very little influence from other breeds.

Height 13–14.2 hands
Colors Dun with dark dorsal stripe

Working horses

Horses can be fast and elegant, but they are also immensely strong. Properly harnessed, they can haul astonishingly heavy loads, and we still use the word *horsepower* as a measure of how much work an engine can do. Before the development of motor vehicles, working horses were a vital part of daily life, and they are still ideal for some tasks.

Draft horses

Horses were used for haulage long before people learned how to ride them. The most basic system is to strap a pack to the back of a horse, but it can shift far more weight if it is harnessed to a vehicle of some sort. Good harness design is vital, although it varies according to the task. Strength is obviously an asset, especially for heavy work, and a typical draft horse is a muscular, even-tempered coldblood, bred for pulling heavy loads.

Packhorses

The first horses to be domesticated were probably used as packhorses. They have the advantage that they can negotiate almost any path through rocky, muddy, or swampy terrain, so they don't need any kind of road. They are often strung together in "trains" like these horses and mules carrying planks in Ecuador.

In harness

Haulage requires special harness. At first, this was based on the throat-girth harness used for oxen, but this restricted a horse's breathing. It was superseded by the breast strap—still used for light work—and then the padded collar. This Russian troika sleigh uses both, with the collar harness in the center.

Brute force

The pulling power of these Clydesdale horses is harnessed using the horse collar, developed in the early Middle Ages. Since the load is on the horse's shoulders, it can lean into the work without restricting its breathing. Chains hooked onto the metal hames of the collar take the strain.

On the towpath

In the 18th century, the hauling power of the horse was massively increased by the development of canal networks. A single horse hitched to a canal boat can haul a far greater weight than one harnessed to a wagon. This canal horse in Germany is having no trouble towing a very heavy barge, even though it is a relatively light breed equipped with a breast-strap harness.

Metal rails

The first railways were developed with horses in mind because, as with canals, the smooth rails greatly increased the weight that one horse could haul. Horse-drawn rail transportation survived on urban streetcar lines such as this one on the Isle of Man— pictured in the 1930s but still operating today.

Horse brass

The head is long and lean, with a Roman nose and big eyes

The long neck is slightly arched

A Shire has good, powerful, sloping shoulders

Shire

This magnificent breed is the biggest and most powerful of all horses. Originating in the British Midlands, its colossal strength made it a natural choice for working in the fields and on the roads all over Britain during the 19th and early 20th centuries. During the 1950s, its numbers decreased dramatically, but its impressive appearance and gentle temperament encouraged a revival of interest, and it is now widely used for displays and heavy horse demonstrations.

Heavy work

Hauling a plow through heavy soil is one of the most demanding tasks for a farm horse, but with its immense pulling power, the Shire is more than capable. Its docile nature makes even a pair easy to handle, despite their size. The foot feathering can be a problem, however, in that it picks up mud.

Shire

Shires hold the record for the world's tallest horse. One 19th-century Shire was said to measure 21.2 hands.

Height Typically over 17 hands
Colors Black, brown, bay, or gray

The long, wide, rounded quarters are well muscled and very strong

The body is very deep and broad

The feet should be feathered, but not too densely

Brabant

Virtually purebred for centuries, this Belgian heavy horse is tremendously powerful and very willing.

Height 15.3–17 hands
Colors Mostly roan or chestnut

Clydesdale

The powerful, long-striding Clydesdale was developed as a Scottish version of the Shire, with similar qualities.

Height 16–18 hands
Colors Bay, brown, or gray, with white face

Suffolk Punch

Massively built, but with relatively short, clean legs, this English breed is ideally built for plowing and similar jobs.

Height 16–16.2 hands
Colors Chestnut

On the farm

Some of the first domesticated horses were probably used for hauling crops off the fields, and until recently horses were the main source of power on farms worldwide. Many were used to draw farm carts, but heavy draft horses were also used to cultivate the land, sow the crops, and bring in the harvest. In the developed world, farming is now highly mechanized, but the farm horse still has its uses.

Raw strength

Some foresters use horses for haulage in its most basic form—simply dragging felled trees out of the woods using chains attached to a horse collar. A horse can maneuver between standing trees to reach areas that are not accessible to vehicles, and its hooves do not churn up the ground like tractor wheels.

Heavy load

The horse-drawn wagon is still widely used on small farms that cannot justify the expense of a tractor. For this Romanian farmer gathering up his hay crop, a horse is not only a cheaper alternative, but more practical. If it is sufficiently well trained, it can move along and stop at his spoken command instead of being driven.

Plow team

For centuries, ox teams were used to plow the land, but when the horse collar was invented, farmers could harness the strength of horses. They could work faster than oxen, and for longer each day, partly because horses do not need to rest in order to digest their food like oxen do. This team is taking part in a display in southern England.

Massive horsepower

In the 19th century, agriculture was revolutionized by new machines such as seed drills and mechanical harvesters. Until the 1920s, most of these machines were horse-drawn, but some—especially in the United States—were so big that they needed a lot of horsepower. This 1910 view shows an early combine harvester being hauled by 24 horses and mules.

Round and round

Horses were not just used in the fields. A horse could also be used to power fixed farmyard equipment using a horse gin. As the horse walked around and around, it turned a capstan that could raise water from a well, or rotate a shaft driving a machine such as a grinding mill.

The head has a slightly dished profile, showing Arab influence

The powerful neck is well crested in stallions

Percheron

Famous for its remarkable stamina, the Percheron was developed over many centuries in the La Perche district of northern France. It is unusually elegant for a heavy horse, with a fluent grace that makes it very popular for demanding carriage work. It owes this quality to regular infusions of Arab blood, which have refined the raw power of the local working horses. Lighter and heavier forms are bred for different tasks.

Grace and power

Powerful and docile, the Percheron has always made an excellent farm horse. But its fusion of strength with elegance also make it an ideal choice for more showy applications, and it is in great demand for special events.

Percheron

In the 19th century, Percherons were used to pull heavy horse-drawn buses on the streets of Paris.

Height 15.2–17 hands
Colors Gray or black

The back is short and strong

The legs are very muscular and strong

Unusually for a heavy horse, the feet are not well feathered

Ardennais

With ancient origins in the border country of France and Belgium, the Ardennais is immensely strong and sure-footed.

Height 15–16 hands
Colors Roan, bay, gray, or chestnut

Boulonnais

Arab and Andalusian blood gives this northern French breed a more aristocratic character than most heavy horses.

Height 15–17 hands
Colors Mainly gray; also bay, chestnut

Charioteers

The earliest horse-drawn vehicles were lumbering solid-wheeled carts, first used about 5,000 years ago. But by 2,000 BCE, some genius had invented the lightweight spoked wheel, and this led to the invention of a small, light, fast two-wheeled vehicle—the chariot. Since this was about 1,000 years before people mastered the art of riding, it was a revelation. Suddenly people could travel at high speeds, and the chariot became a symbol of wealth and prestige as well as a fearsome weapon of war. Eventually, it was adopted by the Romans for racing.

Speed machines
The first known chariots were used 4,000 years ago in Kazakhstan, where the remains of their spoked wheels have been found in ritual burials. But the speedy chariot was soon adopted by other civilizations. This bronze model chariot with a single horse was made in ancient China.

Chariot warfare
Long before anyone rode a horse into battle, wars were fought using chariots. Generally manned by a driver and a fighter, they would charge the enemy to terrify and scatter them, and the fighter would then jump off to fight on foot. Chariots were also used to carry archers, as shown in this image of Egyptian pharaoh Ramesses II at the Battle of Kadesh in 1274 BCE—the largest chariot battle of all, involving about 5,000 chariots.

The horses of Ramesses II leading the charge at the Battle of Kadesh

Chariot racing

To the Romans, a chariot was useless for warfare, but ideal for racing. Like a modern sulky, a racing chariot was little more than a pair of wheels with a flimsy body, but it might have four horses. Each charioteer wrapped the reins around his waist so he could use his weight to control the horses, and carried a knife to free himself if he was thrown.

A day at the races

In Rome, the main chariot racing venue was the Circus Maximus, a long oval track that could accommodate 12 racing chariots at a time, each drawn by up to four horses abreast. To amuse the crowd, the charioteers would try to make their opponents crash, often fatally. This image from the 1959 Hollywood epic *Ben Hur* gives an idea of what it might have been like.

Cattle driving

Horses have been used for rounding up and driving cattle and other animals for centuries— most famously by the cowboys of the American West, whose techniques form the basis of the rodeo. Mounted cattle drives are still important in open range country, where the animals are too widely scattered to be rounded up on foot, and the terrain is too rough for vehicles.

Cowboys

The skills of mounted cattle driving were perfected by the cowboys of 19th-century America, who were employed to round up cattle from unfenced open range, sort them, then drive the selected stock vast distances over open country to market. These modern cowboys still use the same methods.

Western riding

Cowboy techniques are derived from the Spanish riding traditions of Mexico. They include employing a deep, wide, solid saddle and broad stirrups, and using long split reins to control the horse by putting light pressure on its neck. The lariat coiled on this cowgirl's saddle is for roping cattle.

Rodeo

Bronco riding is one of many events that make up the showcase of Western riding skills known as a rodeo. Some, such as calf roping, are closely based on the practical techniques used by working cowboys, but others, such as bull riding and barrel racing, are strictly for show.

Traditional Western saddle

Gauchos

On South American ranches, the cowboys are called gauchos. They have their own traditions, including using the bolas—a triple rope with weights on the rope ends—to catch cattle by entangling their legs. But modern gauchos such as this rider use more conventional methods.

The head is short and broad

muscular and well-formed, the neck is slightly arched

The withers are medium to high, and the shoulders deep, sloping, and powerful

Quarter Horse

The most popular American breed, the Quarter Horse was developed in the 18th century for racing over the short, quarter-mile tracks of the time. It was a cross between mustangs of Spanish ancestry and English horses that were forerunners of the Thoroughbred. The result was a horse with tremendous acceleration, but also a strength, agility, and "cow sense" that made it ideal for ranch work—a truly versatile animal.

Rodeo mount
Its intelligence, speed, and excellent balance make the Quarter Horse a favorite for working cattle. This has led to it becoming the natural choice for Western riding competitions such as cutting, calf roping, and the tests of control known as reining.

Quarter Horse

Bred for sprinting, the Quarter Horse is incredibly fast over short distances, capable of more than 53 mph (85 kph).

Height 14.3–16 hands
Colors Any solid color

The quarters are broad, muscular, and very strong, with great driving power

The legs are strong and extremely well formed

Criollo

Feral Spanish horses lived wild on the Argentinian pampas for 300 years before being tamed as the tough, agile Criollo.

Height 14–15 hands
Colors Mostly dun

Australian Stock Horse

A fusion of Anglo-Arab, Quarter Horse, and even Percheron, this versatile breed is used in competitions as well as ranch work.

Height 14.2–16 hands
Colors Any solid color

The story of Mancha and Gato

Two plucky horses who carried Aimé Tschiffely from Buenos Aires to Washington, D.C.

American Indian reservation

UNITED STATES

St. Louis

Washington, D.C.

Mississippi River

Cotton plantations

San Antonio

Laredo

Desert

Gulf of Mexico

San Luis Potosi

Ancient ruins

MEXICO

Mountains

GUATEMALA

pine forests

SAN SALVADOR

San José

Colón

PANAMA

Swamps

Caribbean Sea

Prairies

COLOMBIA

Bogotá

Quito

ECUADOR

Amazon River

Jungle

PERU

Andes

Lima

Forests

CUZCO

BOLIVIA

La Paz

Pacific Ocean

Paraguay River

Iguazú Falls

Alkali flats

ARGENTINA

Atlantic Ocean

Buenos Aires

They didn't look like much—two scruffy, bad-tempered geldings with short necks and ugly faces that had been living wild for 15 years on the open grasslands of Argentina. One was a red and white skewbald, the other a dun. But by completing an astonishing 10,000 mile (16,000 km) journey, this unpromising pair were to prove themselves the toughest horses on earth.

The horses were bought in 1925 by Aimé Tschiffely, a Swiss adventurer with an idea. He aimed to prove that these half-wild Criollos had more grit and stamina than any other breed by riding them all the way from Argentina to the U.S. capital. He called the skewbald Mancha ("the spotted one"), and the dun Gato ("the cat"), saddled them up, and set off. Most people thought he was crazy.

At times, Tschiffely had his own doubts as they picked their way through treacherous swamps, scaled dizzying heights, and crossed terrifying ravines on rickety bridges. But the horses were not daunted, even by near-catastrophe. At one point in the Andes mountains of Peru, Gato lost his footing and slipped off a precipice. Miraculously, he slid into a tree that stopped him from plunging into the abyss. Somehow, Mancha, Tschiffely, and another traveler hauled him back up to safety, and they carried on.

The roads were often nonexistent, or swept away by landslides. In Ecuador, Mancha was leading as Tschiffely walked behind when they reached a yawning gap in the mountain trail. Mancha simply jumped it, so the others had little choice but to do the same—trying to ignore the sheer drop into the valley far below.

The going became easier as the trio headed northeast across the United States. Eventually, after more than three years on the trail, they were given a heroes' welcome in Washington, D.C. Then, Mancha and Gato returned to their home in Argentina—by ship.

A sturdy tree breaks Gato's fall

Criollo horses

The ancestors of this hardy breed were Spanish horses with Arab and Barb blood, brought to Buenos Aires in the 1530s. When the city was destroyed in 1541, they ran free, and generations of life in the wild created the amazingly tough Criollo.

Gaucho saddle

Tschiffely used the traditional saddle of the gauchos—the cowboys of the South American pampas grasslands. With its lightweight structure and sheepskin covering, it was ideal for long hours in the saddle and made a comfortable pillow at night. He also took a pack saddle, swapping them from one horse to another throughout the long ride.

Horses on show

For centuries, horses have been bred and trained to enhance their beauty and performance. Such horses are living, breathing works of art, and to watch one in action is like watching a dancer on the stage. In the past, they were also used in battle, and as symbols of power and wealth.

Conforming to type

The conformation of any horse describes its basic physical form, which is largely defined by its bone structure. Some elements of conformation apply to all horses, but a horse can have good conformation for one purpose, such as racing, and poor conformation for another, such as heavy draft work. Since each breed has been developed for a particular purpose, each one has its own ideal conformation.

Perfectly formed

This Arab stallion illustrates the points of a horse—the parts of its body. It has good conformation, with a fine, small head, dished face, arched neck, strong shoulders, a deep chest, broad quarters, and clean legs. Some features, such as the dished face, are specific to this breed, but you would look for others in any horse.

A swayback is a conformation fault that is usually seen in older horses, but can also appear in young ones—especially if they have been overworked.

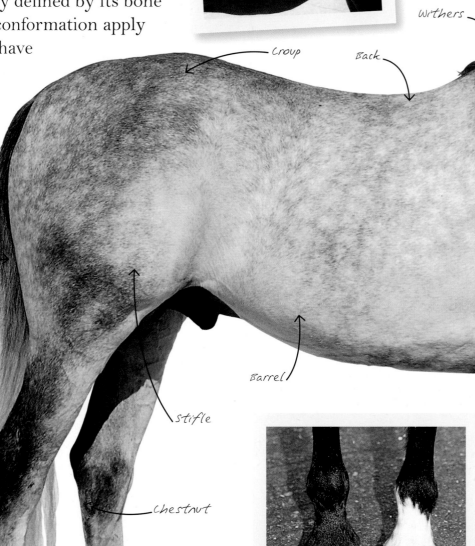

Croup

Back

Withers

Dock

Barrel

Stifle

Chestnut

Hock

Fetlock

Coronet

Heel

A horse with pigeon toes has toes that face in toward each other. This conformation problem puts strain on the lower limbs.

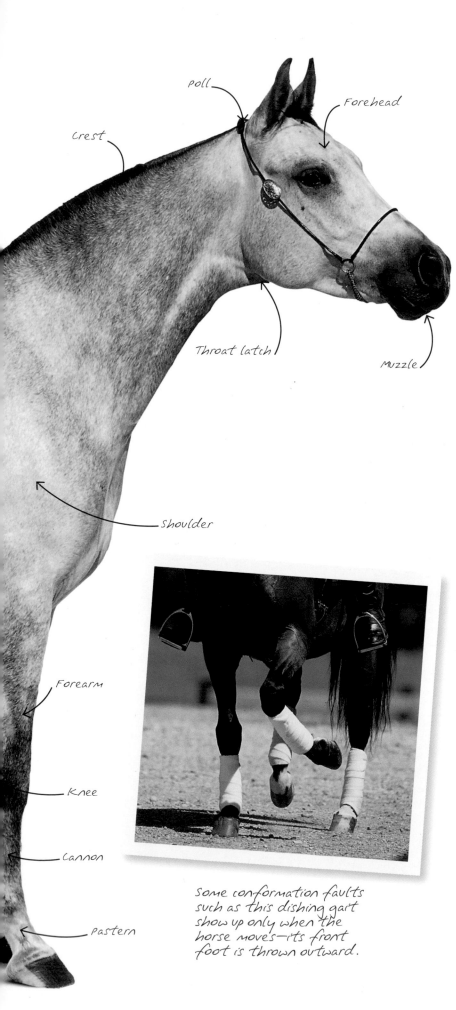

Crest

Poll

Forehead

Throat latch

Muzzle

Shoulder

Forearm

Knee

Cannon

Pastern

Some conformation faults such as this dishing gait show up only when the horse moves—its front foot is thrown outward.

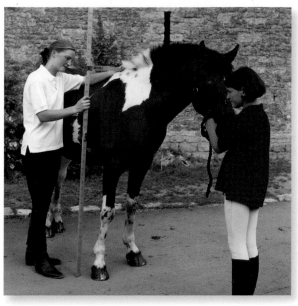

Height

A horse's height is measured from the ground to the top of its withers, often using the "hands" (hh) system. One "hand" is actually four inches (10 cm). A fraction of a hand is given in inches, so a 15.3hh horse is 15 hands and three inches high—not 15 and three-tenths as the "decimal point" implies.

Condition

Bad conformation is not the same thing as poor condition. A horse may have basically excellent conformation, but if it is suffering from lack of exercise, a poor diet, or a health problem, it is likely to be in poor condition. Age is another factor—this 30-year-old Arab gelding was probably a magnificent animal when it was young.

The head is big, with a broad forehead and large eyes.

A thick, well-arched neck carries a very long mane

The shoulders are long and sloping, with prominent withers

Andalusian

One of the oldest, most famous Spanish breeds, the Andalusian is descended from the native wild horses of Andalusia in southern Spain, with a little Arab or Barb blood introduced by medieval Moorish invaders. Purebred in Andalusia for centuries, this athletic, showy horse has contributed to many other breeds, including the Lipizzaner and Lusitano. The Spanish also took the Andalusian to America, where its influence is seen in the Criollo, Quarter Horse, and Appaloosa.

The chest is broad, deep, and well rounded

High school
An Andalusian horse has a spectacular, high-stepping gait and long stride that make it a favorite for demonstrations of "high school" classical dressage. This tradition is maintained at the Royal Andalusian School of Equestrian Art in Jerez de la Frontera, near Cadiz.

Andalusian

Purebred Andalusians almost died out in the early 1800s, but survived at the Cartuja monastery near Seville.

Height 15–16 hands
Colors Gray, bay, black, roan, chestnut

Lusitano

Closely allied to the Andalusian, this Portuguese breed has great strength and poise, and a calm, brave nature.

Height 15–16 hands
Colors Dun, gray, bay, or chestnut

The quarters are muscular, and the legs well proportioned

The lower legs are clean, with very little feathering

Paso Fino

Developed in Puerto Rico during the 16th century, this Spanish-type breed is famous for its smooth, comfortable four-beat gait.

Height 13–15 hands
Colors Any color

79

Black

Brown

Bay

Liver-chestnut

Chestnut

Palomino

Dun

Dapple-gray

Gray

Strawberry-roan

Piebald

Spotted

Star

Snip

Colors and markings

A horse is often described by its color. It might be a chestnut mare, for example, or a black stallion. Many colors, such as roan and dun, are specific to animals such as horses, and even the word gray has a special meaning when applied to horses (see page 102). Some terms such as bay indicate a contrastingly colored mane, tail, and lower limbs—known as the "points"—and any horse may have white markings on its head or legs.

Colors

The main natural horse colors are bay, chestnut, gray, and dun, but these have several variants. There are also many other colors, ranging from solid black to cremello, which is almost albino white. The 12 color types shown on the left are among the most common.

Stripe

Blaze

White face

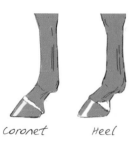

Coronet   Heel

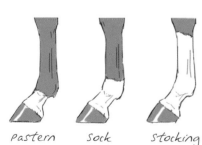

Pastern   Sock   Stocking

Leg markings

Although some horses, such as bays and duns, typically have dark legs, "markings" are always white. Even a bay horse with dark points may have white markings on its legs. There are five main variations, ranging from a narrow white coronet above the hoof to a long stocking, which reaches the knee.

Wall eye

Face markings

As with leg markings, these are always white. There are five basic types—star, snip, stripe, blaze, and white face. Some may be described in more detail, so, for example, a horse might have a faint star or an interrupted stripe. Very extensive markings can sometimes disqualify a horse from registration with a breed society.

Other features

Some horses have "wall eyes," with white or pale blue irises instead of brown. Others have distinctive patterns such as dorsal stripes or leg stripes—both indicating ancient ancestry. A few breeds such as the Appaloosa may even have vertical stripes on their hooves.

Leg stripes

The head is small and lean with a straight profile

Shoulders are long and sloping, with well-defined withers

Appaloosa

Famous for its distinctive spotted coat, the Appaloosa was developed during the 18th century by the Nez Perce people of the Pacific Northwest, who selected high-quality spotted horses from those originally imported by the Spanish. In 1877, the Nez Perce were defeated in the Indian Wars and their horses were dispersed, but the breed has been revived and improved by the injection of Arab, Thoroughbred, and Quarter Horse blood.

The chest is deep, providing good stamina

Elegant mover
The original Appaloosa was bred for stamina, speed, and athleticism, as well as its spots, and its qualities have only been improved by later breeders. It has a very free, smooth, graceful action that makes it good to ride, and it is now one of the most popular American breeds.

The hooves often have vertical black and white stripes

Appaloosa

There are eight basic Appaloosa coat patterns, from plain dark and white to overall white with dark "leopard spots."

Height 14–16 hands
Colors Spotted or two-tone

The legs are strong, and the quarters rounded and powerful

Pony of the Americas

This recent breed was developed in the 1950s from a Shetland-Appaloosa cross. It is docile, elegant, and eye-catching.

Height 11.2–14 hands
Colors Appaloosa patterns

Pinto

Defined by its "painted" pattern rather than its conformation, the Pinto was highly prized by Native American riders.

Height Very variable
Colors Dark and white patches

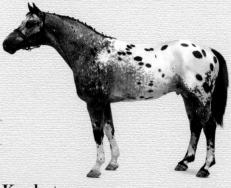

Knabstrup

Developed from a spotted mare brought to Denmark in 1808, this Appaloosa-type breed is a smart, strong riding horse.

Height 15.1–16 hands
Colors Appaloosa pattern on roan base

Native American horses

Although the earliest horses lived in North America, they had died out there by 8,000 BCE, just after the last ice age. They may have been the victims of climate change, but they were also hunted by the ancestors of the American Indians who had moved in from Siberia about 2,000 years earlier. Either way, the wild horses disappeared, so the Native people were not able to domesticate them. But the American Indians got their chance much later, when horses were reintroduced to America by the Spanish, and they soon saw how useful they were.

Spanish horses

Spanish settlers brought horses back to America in the 16th century. They were a mix of breeds, but many had Arab, Barb, and even Lipizzaner blood. When the Pueblo people drove the Spanish back into Mexico in 1680, many horses ran wild, and tribes such as the Pueblo, Apache, and Comanche rounded them up and started riding them.

Tribal revolution

Horses slowly spread east to the Great Plains, where they had a major impact on nomadic tribes such as the Cheyenne. They used them for riding, pulling primitive sleds called travois, carrying goods for exchange with other tribes, hunting, warfare, and horse-stealing raids. Many of the horses they used were stolen from Mexican ranches.

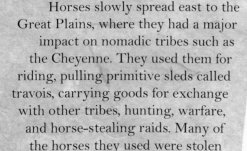

War bridle

Compared to the elaborate tack used by the Spanish, an Indian bridle was very basic. A long piece of rope was looped through the horse's mouth, like a bit, tied around the jaw in a slipknot, then run back as reins. It must have worked well, because the mounted tribal warriors were fearsome in battle.

Roans and Pintos

The horses were of all colors, but each tribe had its favorites. The Sioux preferred chestnuts and roans, and the Nokota horses that run wild in North Dakota have a lot of Sioux blood; many are blue roan. They also liked Pintos and Appaloosas, because the unique pattern of each horse made it easier for its owner to pick it out of the tribal herd.

Native hunters used their horses to get within killing distance of the buffalo herd

Buffalo horses

The most prized horses were those trained for buffalo hunting. It was dangerous work, so the women often decorated them with good-luck symbols. Buffalo horses were so valuable that they were kept by the tepee at night, rather than being left with the other horses where they might be stolen.

Gaits

A horse instinctively uses its legs in different ways to walk, trot, canter, or gallop at a variety of speeds. These are its natural gaits, seen in wild as well as domestic horses. But a horse can also move in ways that are rarely or never seen in wild horses, and which generally have to be learned through artificial training. Many of these specialized gaits are known as "ambling"—a term that covers any gait that is roughly as fast as a trot but much smoother, because the horse has a more even four-beat footfall. This means that they are more comfortable for the rider, especially over very long distances.

Specialized gaits

PACE: Instead of lifting its diagonal front and rear feet as in a trot, the horse lifts both feet on one side at the same time—a lateral gait. Some harness racers are natural pacers.

Natural gaits

WALK: This is the slowest, but steadiest and most comfortable natural gait. It is an even four-beat movement, with each foot lifted and put down in sequence—an action known as a square gait. The horse moves both feet on one side forward, then both feet on the other side, but it always has two or three feet on the ground.

TROT: A trotting horse springs from one diagonal to the other with a steady two-beat action, placing both diagonally opposite feet on the ground at once. In between these footfalls, all four feet are in the air. For a rider, trotting is made more comfortable by rising from the saddle every other beat—a technique known as posting.

TÖLT: Practiced mainly by Icelandic Horses, this four-beat gait is like a walk, but with a higher action and more speed. It is smooth and very comfortable for the rider.

RACK: This is the speciality of the American Saddlebred—a very even, four-beat lateral gait that is as fast as trotting or pacing, but smoother and more showy.

RUNNING WALK: A Tennessee Walker has a fast, even four-beat square gait that has been described as trotting with its front feet while walking with its hind feet.

CANTER: In this three-beat gait, the horse lifts one hind foot, then simultaneously the other hind foot and opposite front foot, and finally the other front foot. Since the action starts at the back and leads to the front, it causes a rocking motion. This sequence will finish on the near (left) front foot, but the horse can swap from one side to the other.

GALLOP: Galloping is similar to cantering, but the horse moves its legs one at a time to create a four-beat movement, starting at the back and finishing at the front, followed by a moment when all four hooves are in the air. This is the fastest gait, but the most tiring—a typical horse can keep up a gallop for only about eight minutes.

The Peruvian Paso always carries its head high

The muscular neck has a prominent crest

Long, sloping shoulders permit a long stride

Peruvian Paso

Also called the Peruvian Stepping Horse, this elegant breed was derived from Spanish horses brought to Peru by Francisco Pizarro in the 1530s. It combines Barb and Andalusian blood with a hint of Spanish Jennet—a breed known for its four-beat "broken pace." The Peruvian Paso inherited this, and over four centuries of selective breeding it has been refined into a uniquely smooth, fast gait that the horse can maintain for long distances over rough terrain.

Stepping gait

Instead of trotting, a Peruvian Paso lifts each foot in turn in a variation of the pace, with the left hindfoot followed by left forefoot, then right hindfoot and right forefoot. In doing so, it swings its forelegs out in an arc. This action absorbs footfall shock, giving a very comfortable ride.

Long legs are used in an energetic, high-stepping fashion

Peruvian Paso

Both the gait and action of this breed
are completely natural, and are
inherited by all of its offspring.

Height 14.2–15.2 hands
Colors Usually chestnut or bay

Very muscular
quarters power
the horse's
action

The body
is broad
and deep

American Saddlebred

This intelligent, versatile breed is often
trained to perform artificial four-beat
gaits in addition to its natural gaits.

Height 15–16 hands
Colors Any solid color

Missouri Fox Trotter

Like the Peruvian Paso, this was bred for
quickly covering long distances, walking
with its forelegs and trotting behind.

Height 14–16 hands
Colors Any color

Tennessee Walker

Known for its three unusual but natural
gaits, this is both a very comfortable
mount and a spectacular show horse.

Height 15–16 hands
Colors Chestnut, black, bay, or roan

Horse-drawn carriages

For centuries, horse-drawn vehicles were the main form of wheeled transportation all over the world. They evolved into a host of designs with wonderful names such as curricle, phaeton, brougham, and landau. The main division is between two-wheelers, which are mostly open vehicles, and heavier four-wheelers with closed or convertible coachwork, which are often hauled by teams of horses.

Traps and gigs
Light, maneuverable two-wheelers are usually pulled by a single horse between shafts. Most have springs for comfort, and many have a folding hood to provide some protection from the weather. A dashboard shields the driver and passengers from dirt kicked up by the horse.

Royal opulence

Built for King George III in 1762, and sheathed with real gold, the Gold State Coach of British royalty is one of the most spectacular horse-drawn carriages in the world. It is so heavy that it requires an eight-horse team driven by four riders known as postillions.

Four-wheelers

Many four-wheeled carriages like this landau have a sheltered body for the passengers and an open "box" for the driver. Some wealthy owners used matched four-horse teams, but a pair was more typical, harnessed to a swiveling front axle that enables the vehicle to negotiate corners.

Teams and harness

Carriage horses are often used singly, but may also be harnessed in pairs, four-in-hand, or even in tandem like this. For light work, the strain is taken by breast straps rather than collars, and the horse or horses nearest the vehicle are harnessed with breeching straps so they can slow it down.

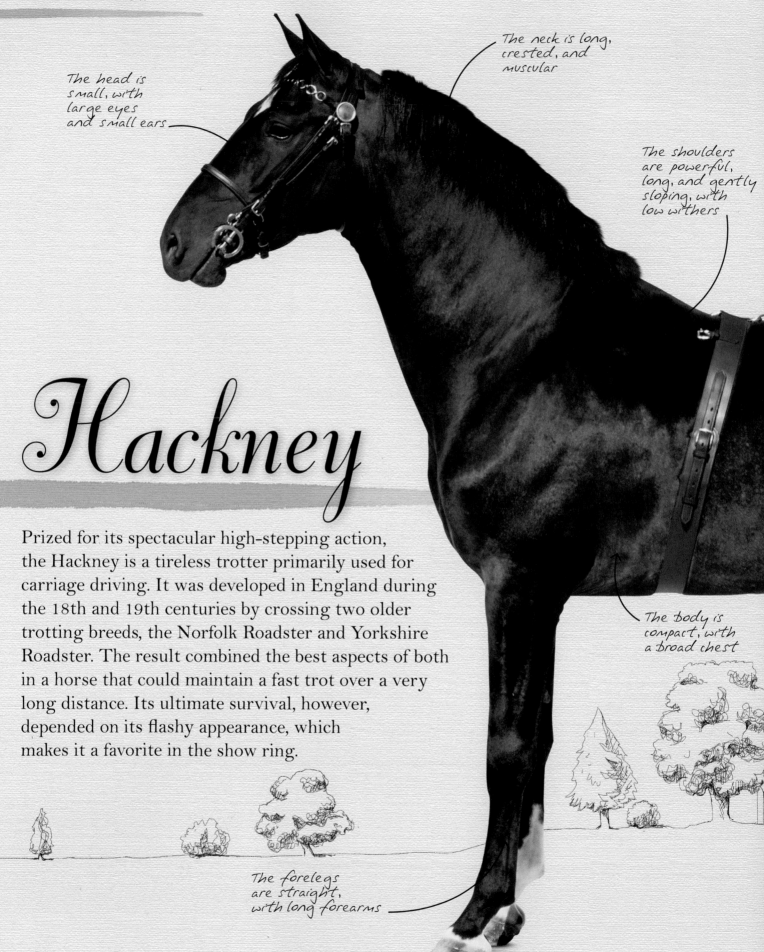

The neck is long, crested, and muscular

The head is small, with large eyes and small ears

The shoulders are powerful, long, and gently sloping, with low withers

Hackney

Prized for its spectacular high-stepping action, the Hackney is a tireless trotter primarily used for carriage driving. It was developed in England during the 18th and 19th centuries by crossing two older trotting breeds, the Norfolk Roadster and Yorkshire Roadster. The result combined the best aspects of both in a horse that could maintain a fast trot over a very long distance. Its ultimate survival, however, depended on its flashy appearance, which makes it a favorite in the show ring.

The body is compact, with a broad chest

The forelegs are straight, with long forearms

Hackney Pony

First created by crossing a Hackney stallion with Fell pony mares in the 1880s, this is a tough but elegant driving pony. It has an even more extravagant action than its larger relative, raising its knees very high to create a dramatic effect when trotting in harness.

The tail is carried high

The quarters are very strong

Hackney

The name Hackney may derive from the French word *haquenée*, meaning "horse for hire."

Height 14–16 hands
Colors Any solid color

Morgan

Founded by a single fine stallion in the 1790s, this American breed combines class with strength and stamina.

Height 14.1–15.2 hands
Colors Any solid color

Oldenburger

Originally developed as a tall, powerful carriage horse in northwest Germany, this breed has been adapted for riding.

Height 16.1–17.2 hands
Colors Bay, brown, black, or gray

Orlov Trotter

This elegant Russian breed was created for harness racing in the late 18th century, and has great endurance.

Height 16–17 hands
Colors Gray, black, or bay

The story of the Pony Express

and Sylph, the little chestnut mare who blazed the trail

Sylph leaves St. Joseph in a cloud of dust

On a warm April evening in 1860, the streets of St. Joseph, Missouri, were packed with people cheering a young rider named Johnny Fry and his pretty chestnut mare, Sylph. There were speeches and applause as he was given a leather pouch of letters bound for San Francisco, half a continent away to the west. At 7:15, a gun fired—and Sylph galloped off on the first-ever journey of the Pony Express.

Luckily for Sylph, she didn't have to make the whole 1,900 mile (3,000 km) trip across America. The Pony Express was a gigantic relay race involving 400 horses and 120 riders. They rode day and night along rough trails, carrying the precious mail between 184 relay stations, where they would change horses and often carry on. They suffered searing heat and icy blizzards, and fought off attacks by hostile Native tribes.

Each rider had to cover at least 80 miles (130 km) at a fast trot or canter—or a gallop if he hit trouble. They needed a fresh mount every 12 miles (20 km) or so, leaving the tired pony at the relay station to recover. But things could go badly wrong. On one occasion, 16-year-old Bill Cody outrode a group of armed Native warriors only to find the staff of the relay post lying dead and all the horses stolen. He had to keep going on the same horse, covering 24 miles (40 km) at punishing speed.

The Pony Express route ended in Sacramento, California, and the mail was then carried downriver by ferryboat to San Francisco. The journey took 10 days. It was an amazing undertaking, made possible by brave men and brave ponies. But it only lasted 18 months, because in October 1861 engineers completed an electric telegraph system that allowed messages to be flashed across the continent in a few minutes.

At the western end, the route crossed rugged mountains

Hostile tribes made the route over the plains very dangerous

The route from the east started where the railroad ended

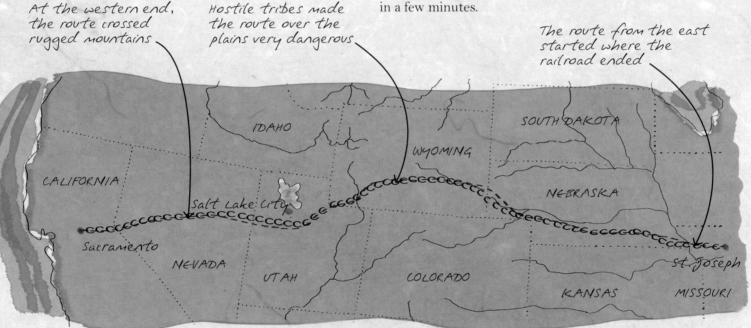

PONY EXPRESS ROUTE, 1860

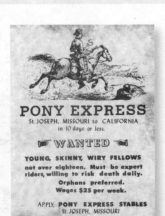

Young riders

Pony Express riders were very young. This recruiting poster asks for "young, wiry fellows, not over 18." They had to be "willing to risk death daily"—and it even says "orphans preferred"! But they were paid well, earning 25 times the normal wage of the time.

Fast and tough

The mounts ranged from big cavalry horses such as Morgans at the eastern end of the route, to tamed mustangs at the western end. Pinto ponies were often used on the Great Plains section, which was unfortunate because the Native warriors liked them too, and often stole them.

Riding into battle

Horses have been ridden into battle since Scythians terrorized the ancient world during the late Bronze Age, almost 3,000 years ago. The invention of stirrups around 500 BCE made cavalry even more effective, and they remained a devastating weapon until the eve of World War I. But mechanized warfare soon made mounted troops redundant, and today their skills are reserved for ceremonial parades.

Mounted archers
Some riders were armed with swords and lances, but others carried bows. The skill of mounted archery was perfected by the Japanese samurai, and it survives as a martial art called *yabusame*, in which the archer gallops at high speed while shooting at three targets in quick succession.

Embroidered horsemen
In 1066, English footsoldiers were defeated at the Battle of Hastings by the Norman army, largely because of the power of their cavalry. In the 1070s, the event was vividly depicted on the Bayeux Tapestry, which clearly shows the force of the Norman cavalry charge.

Lancers and dragoons

By the 18th and 19th centuries, many nations had cavalry regiments with different functions, including lancers, who fought with lances (spears), and dragoons, who carried short rifles. Like many soldiers of the period, they had splendid, often vividly colored uniforms designed to overawe their enemies. Typical cavalry horses were middleweight mares and geldings of about 15 hands.

Cavalry helmet with white plume

16th-century cavalry sword

Parade drill

The cavalry relied on disciplined tactics to maintain control of their horses under fire. These were drilled into the troops by relentless training in precise maneuvers. Light cavalry preferred speed and agility in their horses, while armored cavalry needed strength. Now obsolete in warfare, cavalry horses form part of parades such as the royal Trooping the Colour ceremony held in London.

Cleveland Bay

This is one of the oldest British breeds, dating back to the Middle Ages. Developed as a packhorse in Cleveland, northeast England, it became a popular carriage horse before going into decline in the early 20th century. It has since recovered, largely because its cause was taken up by the British royal family, and it is widely used to improve other breeds.

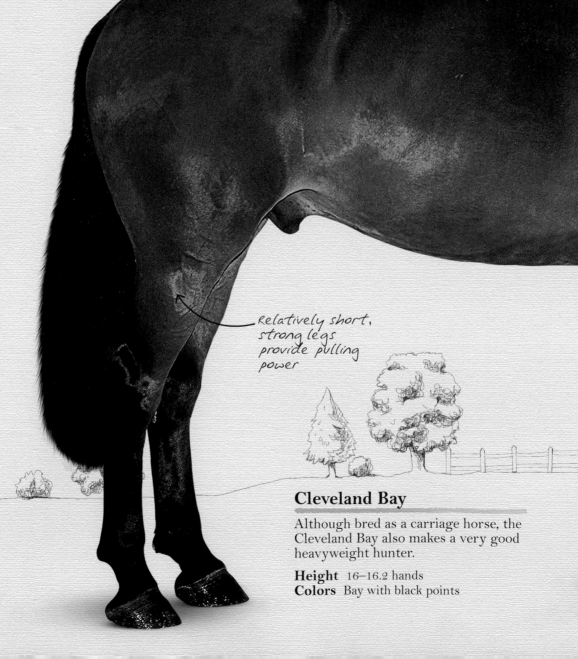

Relatively short, strong legs provide pulling power

Cleveland Bay

Although bred as a carriage horse, the Cleveland Bay also makes a very good heavyweight hunter.

Height 16–16.2 hands
Colors Bay with black points

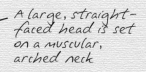

The ears are long and expressive

A large, straight-faced head is set on a muscular, arched neck

The shoulders are sloping, deep, and very powerful

Gelderlander

Developed in the Netherlands for farm work, this versatile breed is now often used in competitive driving events.

Height 15.2–16.2 hands
Colors Usually chestnut

Don

Originating on the Russian steppes, the Don is an incredibly hardy breed once used by Cossack cavalry, but also driven.

Height 15.2–16.2 hands
Colors Usually chestnut or bay

Class act

By 1962, the Cleveland Bay had declined to the point that just four breeding stallions were left. It was saved from extinction at least partly through royal patronage, and is now the main carriage horse used by the royal stables in London. Here, a team of Cleveland Bays has been prepared for a state parade.

Budenny

This relatively new Russian breed was created during the Soviet era as a cavalry horse, but is also an excellent jumper.

Height 15.2–16.1 hands
Colors Chestnut, bay, brown, or gray

Classical riding

During the Middle Ages, horses were generally trained using harsh and even brutal methods. But from the 16th century onward, trainers rediscovered more humane techniques developed long ago in Ancient Greece. These were taught in high-class riding schools to create the art of classical riding—a demonstration of obedience, precision, refinement, and matchless style.

Ancient wisdom
The main elements of classical riding come from a book called *On Horsemanship*, created by the Ancient Greek writer Xenophon around 360 BCE. This image on a pot dates from that same era. Xenophon's training methods were based on kindness and reward, and when trainers started using them again, they found them very effective.

Classical revival
In the 18th century, cavalries started using faster but more temperamental horses such as Andalusians. This led to a surge of interest in classical horsemanship and training. In 1733, François Robichon de la Guérinière (right) published *École de cavalerie* ("School of Cavalry"), which became the key text on the subject.

Airs above ground
De la Guérinière's methods were developed into classical riding techniques designed to increase a horse's athleticism. They include the theatrical "airs above ground" such as the corbette (top), levade (middle), and capriole (bottom). A horse must go through intense training to perform these well.

Leather boots

Gloves to aid grip

The Spanish Riding School

The most famous classical training center is the Spanish Riding School in Vienna, where riding exhibitions are held in the ornate 18th-century indoor Winter Riding School. The horses are all Lipizzaner stallions, ridden without stirrups, and the riders wear Napoleonic-era uniforms.

Lipizzaner

This strikingly athletic breed is famous as the only horse used for classical dressage at the Spanish Riding School in Vienna. The name of the school reflects the horse's Spanish origins—the breed is descended from Andalusians acquired by Austrian Archduke Charles II in 1580 to establish a stud at Lipizza (now Lipica in Slovenia). Other breeds were also used, but mainly of Spanish type. Since 1920, the school's horses have been purebred at Piber, Austria, with rigorous selection for quality.

The breed has muscular, sloping shoulders and a long back

The quarters are rounded, with a well-set tail

The strong legs have broad joints and small, tough feet

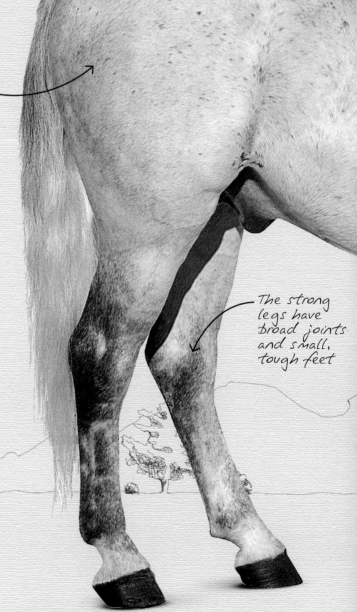

Older and grayer
Although some Lipizzaners are bay, the vast majority are gray. Like all gray horses, they have white hair, black skin, and dark eyes, and when they are born their coat is dark too. Over the years, their hair becomes paler until they become almost entirely white between six and ten years of age.

Lipizzaner

The original Lipizzaners have survived several wars. In 1945, they were at risk of being slaughtered for meat by Soviet forces, but the U.S. Army rescued them.

Height 15–16 hands
Colors Gray, but occasionally bay

The head is long, with a deep jaw and large eyes

The arched neck is short and sturdy, with relatively flat withers and a wide, deep chest

Similar breed

Alter Real

The Portuguese version of the Lipizzaner is also based on Andalusian blood. It has an extremely springy, athletic action.

Height 15–16 hands
Colors Mainly bay, brown, or gray

Sport horses

Most horses are bred for use in races or sporting events. Some are incredibly fast, others have terrific jumping ability, and a few have amazing endurance. They can be trained to perform faultlessly in the arena, or on the polo field. But for most riders, their sport is not about competing, but simply enjoying the ride.

Racing and jump racing

Racing on horseback is probably as old as riding itself. The Romans certainly enjoyed it, and informal races were held throughout the Middle Ages. Over time, these contests developed into events with strict rules, now run on dedicated tracks by horses that are specially bred for speed. Some are straightforward flat races, while others involve jumping over various types of fences.

Over the fences

The most famous jump races are run over racecourses with specially built fences. They include the British Grand National, the Virginia Gold Cup, and Le Grand Steeple-Chase de Paris. More hazardous than flat races, they are often run in winter when the softer ground makes a fall less dangerous.

Flat racing

Racing on a track with no jumps can vary from a flat-out sprint over a short distance to an endurance event that takes a lot of stamina as well as sheer speed. Some races, such as the Melbourne Cup in Australia, are run on grass, while others, like this Thoroughbred championship in Texas, are run on dirt tracks. In Britain, racing became the "sport of kings," patronized by a succession of monarchs. In 1660, Charles II encouraged regular racing at Newmarket, and later Queen Anne set up a course at Ascot.

Steeplechasing

Racing over jumps originated in Ireland in 1752 as a cross-country race from one church steeple to another, jumping any hedges and gates that barred the way. It was known as steeplechasing, and similar point-to-point races are still popular with amateur riders.

Horses and jockeys
Most top-level racehorses are Thoroughbreds, ridden by light jockeys to reduce weight. For speed and freedom of movement, they ride high off the horse's back, leaning forward on very short stirrups, so they need to be very strong with outstanding balance.

The story of Seabiscuit

The legendary racehorse who warmed the hearts of Americans during the Great Depression

The atmosphere was electric, with at least 40,000 spectators crammed into the Baltimore racecourse for the "Match of the Century"—a head-to-head race between the Triple Crown champion War Admiral and California challenger Seabiscuit. It was November 1938, and the United States was in the grip of the deepest depression of the 20th century. People were hungry for heroes, and Seabiscuit was a star.

War Admiral was famous for being quick off the mark, and two-horse races favor fast starters. But Seabiscuit had been secretly trained to catapult off the line when he heard the starting bell. He swept into the lead, and held it until the back stretch when War Admiral drew level. Across the country, four million people crouched by their radios, barely able to breathe. Then, as the horses entered the final straight, Seabiscuit surged ahead to win by four clear lengths. The crowd went wild.

When car magnate Charles Howard bought Seabiscuit in 1936, the bay Thoroughbred seemed to be just an average racehorse. But Howard's racing trainer knew this horse was special, and hired experienced jockey Red Pollard to ride him. Within a few months, the pair were inseparable, and in 1937 they won 11 of the 15 races they entered. But in early 1938, Pollard had two bad accidents, and it was his friend George Woolf who rode Seabiscuit against War Admiral. Disaster struck again when Seabiscuit tore a ligament in his front left leg, and it looked like his racing career was over.

Desperate not to lose his precious horse, Howard sent Seabiscuit to his California ranch to join the injured Pollard. Throughout 1939, the pair recovered together, slowly learning to walk, then trot, then gallop. Pollard had to wear a brace on his weak leg, but he was determined to race again—and race on Seabiscuit.

By 1940, they were ready, and in March they entered the richest race in the California racing calendar—the Santa Anita Handicap. Seabiscuit had never won it before. Could he win it now? He certainly had the fighting spirit, and all America was rooting for him. By the halfway mark, he seemed trapped in third place, but as 78,000 spectators cheered him on, he burst into the lead, streaking ahead to win by a length and a half. Already a champion, Seabiscuit had now become a legend.

Top trainer

Seabiscuit was trained by Tom Smith, a man well known for turning ordinary horses into winners. He saw Seabiscuit's potential and persuaded Howard to buy him. "Get me that horse," he told his boss. "He has real stuff in him. I can improve him. I'm positive." He was right.

Racing legend

Just days after his stunning win at the 1940 Santa Anita Handicap, Seabiscuit retired from racing for good. He became a breeding stallion at his owner's ranch, siring an amazing 108 "little biscuits." In June 2007, a statue of Seabiscuit was unveiled at the ranch, commemorating one of racing's greatest champions.

Thoroughbred

The Thoroughbred is the ultimate racehorse, now bred throughout the world, but originally developed in Britain by crossing local horses with Arabs, Barbs, and others. In fact, the bloodline of every Thoroughbred now alive can be traced back to three stallions active in England from 1690 to the 1730s: the Byerley Turk—possibly an Akhal-Teke—the Darley Arabian, and the Godolphin Arabian (a Barb). Other imported horses were also involved until 1770, after which breeders simply selected for quality and sheer speed. The result is an undisputed champion.

The back is short, but the quarters are muscular and extremely strong

Winning form

Over anything other than the shortest distance, the Thoroughbred is the fastest horse on Earth. This also makes it the most valuable, with vast sums paid for proven performers that may breed future winners.But Thoroughbreds are also crossed with less hot-blooded breeds to create excellent horses 0for general riding.

Thoroughbred

The Thoroughbred is known for its flighty, hot-blooded temperament, and usually needs an experienced rider.

Height 15–17 hands
Colors Most solid colors

The Thoroughbred has high withers, sloping shoulders, and a very deep chest

The refined, elegant head is set on an arched neck

The legs are long and clean

The pasterns are long, and the hooves well shaped

Similar breed

Anglo-Arab

Basically an Arab-Thoroughbred cross, the Anglo-Arab is bred mainly in France as a fast but tough eventing horse.

Height 15.2–16.3 hands
Colors Most solid colors

111

Equine movie stars

Many movies feature horses in starring roles, and the horse-centred Western has been a mainstay of American television for more than 60 years. The drama often requires horses to perform in particular ways and work with the camera crew, so they must be trained for the job. This takes time and the expertise of specialized trainers, so any horse that has been trained for one movie is a natural choice for another. As a result some horses have appeared in a number of films, taking different roles. They are movies stars, even if they don't know it.

Opera stars

Western movies are sometimes known as "horse operas," and for good reason— horses are a major part of the action. Most of the horses were nameless, but some classic Western series were based on one man and his horse. Roy Rogers and Trigger, seen here, made many films together. Several other stars also rode favorite horses. John Wayne had Beau, and James Stewart rode Pie in a partnership that lasted 22 years.

Action hero

In *The Mask of Zorro* (1998), set in the Spanish-ruled California of the 1820s, a mysterious black-clad swordsman defends the rights of the people against their tyrannical rulers. His horse, Toronado, was played by a black Friesian stallion named Casey, who, according to his trainer, was "an exceptional animal actor." Along with other horses used in the movie, he performs several dramatic stunts, such as climbing stairs and apparently jumping across rooftops, as his rider carries out daring rescue missions.

George wears the armor of a Roman general's horse

Zorro's horse, Toronado, was jet black, so they couldn't be seen at night

Imperial charger

The Imperial Roman epic *Gladiator* (2000) stars Russell Crowe as a powerful general reduced to fighting for his life in the circus arena. In the early scenes, he rides a striking black Andalusian named George, who has appeared in several other big movies. His screen presence and experience have made him one of the most sought-after equine stars.

Chestnut superstar

When Julia Roberts was filming the title role of *Runaway Bride* (1999), she rode a chestnut Thoroughbred-Quarter Horse cross named Hightower. She liked him so much that she had him flown across the country for the final shoot rather than ride a substitute. Hightower also starred as Pilgrim in *The Horse Whisperer* (1998), and as Ginger in a 1994 version of *Black Beauty*.

Racing on wheels

Competing in horse-drawn vehicles has an even longer history than flat racing, going back to the earliest chariot races. Modern competitive driving ranges from racing light two-wheeled sulkies at high speeds, to carriage driving with up to four in hand. Many competitions are designed to test control and maneuverability rather than sheer speed, and some encourage drivers to compete in traditional vehicles and flamboyant period clothing.

Combined driving

In this three-day event, up to four horses harnessed to a light carriage compete in a dressage stage, a fast and hazardous cross-country stage—complete with water obstacles—and a test of accuracy that involves negotiating a course laid out with cones. It demands great driving skill.

Harness racing

Fast and exciting, harness races take place on oval tracks resembling regular racecourses. The horses either trot or pace according to the race rules, and their drivers use tactics to conserve their energy before going for a sprint finish.

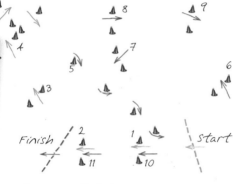

Scurry driving

This is a test of high-speed maneuverability for light four-wheelers drawn by two ponies or horses. The aim is to drive as fast as possible around a course marked out by pairs of cones without hitting any. The driver's partner has to work hard, leaning into the corners to keep the scurry from flipping over.

Chuckwagon racing

Popular in Canada, this rodeo event for up to four teams uses wagons modeled on those that carried food and cooking gear for cowboys on long cattle drives. At the start, outriders load a stove and tent poles onto the wagons, which must then complete a tight figure-eight course before racing around a track to the finish line.

Standardbred

If the Thoroughbred is the fastest mounted racehorse, the Standardbred is the fastest harness racer. It was developed in the United States from various trotting or pacing breeds crossed with Thoroughbreds, especially the English stallion Messenger, who was brought to America in 1788. Many decades of selective breeding since then have created a sturdy, willing, and very fast horse with natural pacing ability, often used to upgrade other breeds.

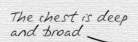

The chest is deep and broad

Similar breeds

French Trotter

Although developed as a harness racer like the Standardbred, this is a more robust breed, and never paces.

Height Average 16.1 hands
Colors Any solid color

Friesian

This glamorous Dutch driving horse has a long history, and is well known for its spectacular high-stepping trot.

Height 14.3–15.3 hands
Colors Black

Trotters and pacers

Harness racing is very different from flat racing, because the horses trot or pace rather than gallop. A Standardbred may do either, but rarely both. The breed gets its name from a "standard" laid down by the breed society in 1879, requiring a qualifying horse to trot a mile (1.6 km) in two and a half minutes.

The back is long, with powerful quarters and strong shoulders

The legs are powerful but shorter than a Thoroughbred's, with very strong feet

Standardbred

Apart from racing, Standardbreds are often used as light carriage horses, especially by the Amish people.

Height 14–16 hands
Colors Bay, brown, or chestnut

Dressage

Competitive dressage is a test of a horse's training, obedience, and style. It is based on the classical riding tradition seen at the Spanish Riding School in Vienna, and puts the same emphasis on precision and elegance. Although it can seem highly artificial, it is actually all about the most basic riding skills: getting the horse moving properly and doing exactly what you want.

Precision riding

Dressage involves riding a set series of movements with names such as the passage, half-pass, extended trot, pirouette, and piaffe. Each competitor's performance is judged on the horse's responsiveness to the slightest command, its obedience and precision, and the general appearance of horse and rider.

White gloves and top hat

Spick and span

All breeds of horse are eligible for dressage competitions, but the horse must be impeccably turned out, with a clean coat, oiled hooves, plaited mane, and pulled tail. High-level riders wear top hats, white gloves, tail coats, white riding breeches, high boots, and spurs.

Prix Caprilli

This contest is a dressage test with jumps, named after Captain Federico Caprilli (1868–1907), the Italian cavalry instructor who invented the forward jumping seat. There are usually just two very low jumps, designed to test the horse's action and gaits as well as the rider's style.

Leg control

Dressage riders use longer stirrups than normal, allowing them to ride with their knees relaxed and only slightly bent. This gives them excellent control, because it increases their ability to communicate with the horse by feel and touch. Guiding the horse in this subtle fashion is one of the main skills of dressage.

Reining

This is a Western form of dressage that involves using a light, one-handed touch on the reins and subtle leg control to guide the horse through a precise pattern of circles, spins, and stops. The tests, such as this sliding stop, are much faster and more dramatic than in dressage—and the dress code is completely different!

Dutch Warmblood

A relatively new breed created in the 1960s, the Dutch Warmblood was developed as a sport horse that combines winning performance with a calm, disciplined temperament. Hotblood stallions such as Thoroughbreds and Arabs were crossed with the local Groningen and Gelderlander working breeds to create a horse with the best qualities of both, and since the breed was established, a system of rigorous testing has ensured that only the finest animals are used as breeding stock.

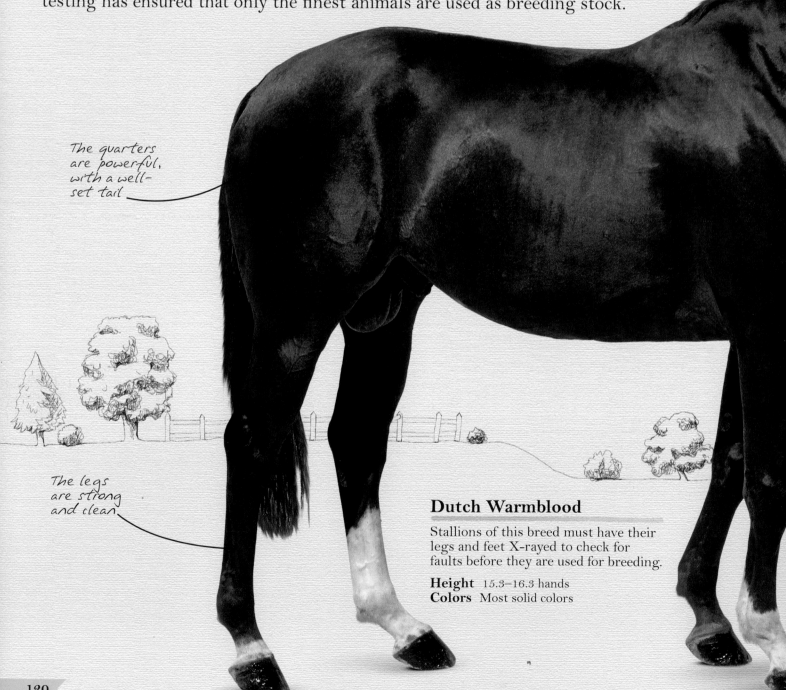

The quarters are powerful, with a well-set tail

The legs are strong and clean

Dutch Warmblood

Stallions of this breed must have their legs and feet X-rayed to check for faults before they are used for breeding.

Height 15.3–16.3 hands
Colors Most solid colors

The well-shaped head has a broad forehead

The neck is muscular and well proportioned

Danish Warmblood

Similar to its Dutch counterpart, the Danish Warmblood was bred from local Frederiksborgs and Holsteiners crossed with Thoroughbreds.

Height 15.3–17 hands
Colors Most solid colors

Horses for courses

Dutch Warmbloods excel at competitive sports. Recently, some strains have become specialized for particular events, especially dressage and show jumping, which require horses with different qualities. But the strains are still interbred to maintain overall quality.

Hanoverian

Created in the 18th century as an all-purpose breed, this has been converted into a fine jumping and dressage horse.

Height 15.3–17 hands
Colors Most solid colors

Show jumping

When horses race over fences, each spectator can watch only one obstacle at a time. But in the 19th century, people started laying out jumping courses in arenas, so everyone could see all the action as each horse tried to clear all the fences in the right order. Such events can be staged indoors, rain or shine, and are ideal for television coverage—making show jumping one of the most popular equestrian sports.

Long and high

There are up to 14 fences in each course, designed to look like walls, hedges, plank barriers, or poles. They can all be knocked down if not cleared cleanly. Many are high, but others are long-jump spreads or combination fences. There may also be a water jump, like this one in Guadalajara, Mexico.

Fault!

Show jumping events vary in format, but basically the competitors attempt the course one at a time, aiming for a clear round within a set time. If they succeed, they go on to compete in a jump-off against the clock. They are judged purely on performance, with faults incurred for refusals and knockdowns like this.

Forward seat

Show jumpers use shorter stirrups than usual, enabling them to adopt a forward position that helps the jumping horse's balance. Most horses wear tough boots to protect the tendons of their lower legs, and the saddle girth often has a belly guard for protection against the studs that are used on their shoes to improve grip.

Winning rosette

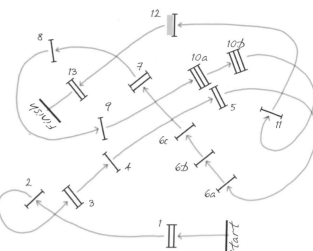

Course design

The course is arranged so that the horses can make a certain number of strides between each fence—including half strides at higher levels. They may also approach some jumps at an angle. At least one of the jumps is a combination fence, with two or three fences in quick succession, as in fence 6 above.

Over the wall

One form of show jumping, puissance, is all about the height of the fences. Its main feature is the "puissance wall," with kick-out blocks resembling solid masonry. During jump-offs, there are just two obstacles—a spread fence and the wall—but they are raised for each round and the wall can reach 6.6 ft (2 m) or more.

Selle Français

Famous for its prowess as a show jumper, the Selle Français is a development of a breed known as the Anglo-Norman. This was essentially a cross between the local horses of Normandy and imported Thoroughbred, Norfolk Trotter, and Arab stallions. Creating the Selle Français involved crossing the Anglo-Norman with several other regional breeds and yet more Thoroughbred blood to develop an excellent sport horse. But the breed includes a wide range of types bred for different disciplines.

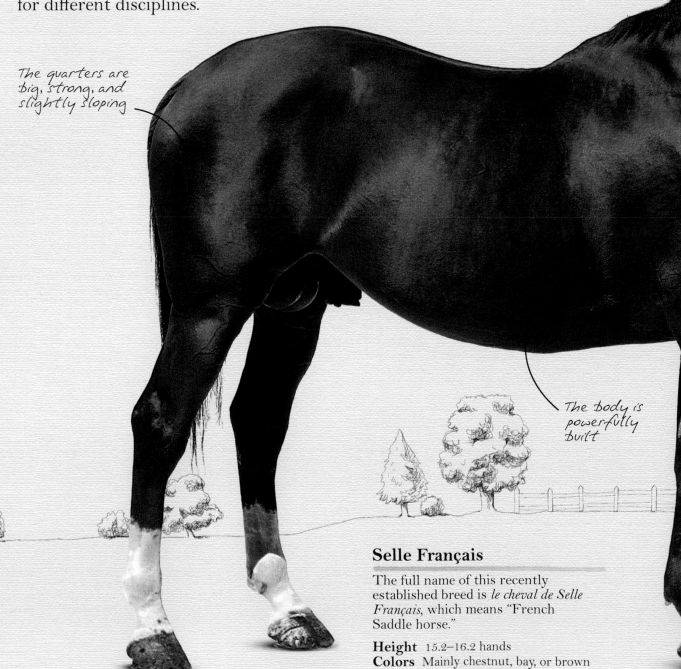

The quarters are big, strong, and slightly sloping

The body is powerfully built

Selle Français

The full name of this recently established breed is *le cheval de Selle Français*, which means "French Saddle horse."

Height 15.2–16.2 hands
Colors Mainly chestnut, bay, or brown

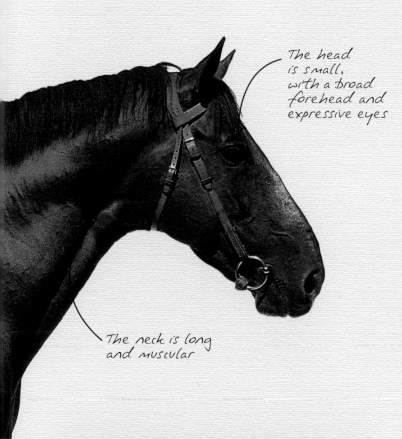

The head is small, with a broad forehead and expressive eyes

The neck is long and muscular

Holsteiner

Once a military and carriage horse, this north German breed has now been refined into a world-class show jumper.

Height 16–17 hands
Colors Any solid color

Champion jumper

There are three main types of Selle Français, bred for general riding, racing, or eventing. The last are the most valuable, because their athleticism and boldness makes them excellent show jumpers. One horse of this breed won the show jumping World Cup an unprecedented three years in a row.

Westphalian

Another German warmblood, this is a superb show jumper—but it has also done well in dressage and driving events.

Height 15.2–16.2 hands
Colors Any solid color

Eventing

Equestrian events are competitions that are designed to test a horse's stamina, speed, agility, and training. In their simplest form, known as horse trials or hunter trials, each competitor tackles a cross-country jumping course. Eventing combines this with show jumping and dressage stages, making for a much more demanding competition that calls for mastery of a wide range of skills on the part of both horse and rider.

Horse trials

Horse trials take place over cross-country courses that involve jumping a variety of fairly modest fences. There are different classes designed to cater to varying levels of skill, so horse trials are an ideal introduction to more challenging competitions such as eventing.

A horse should jump the narrowest part of a "corner" fence

Artificial hedge

Staged contest

More difficult than horse trials, eventing combines dressage, show jumping, and cross-country jumping stages, which take place over one to four days. The dressage stage is not as exacting as a pure dressage competition; its aim is to test the horse's agility, obedience, and temperament.

Cross-country challenge

The fences on a cross-country eventing or trials course are as varied as possible, with a range of heights, lengths, and visual challenges. This course includes a water jump, a line of barrels, a log pile, and a set of steps. Many of these "natural obstacles" are designed to break if hit hard to prevent dangerous falls.

Classic events

Eventing is a highly charged sport that attracts world-class riders. Here, Brook Staples and top international eventer Daws Willowherb negotiate the water jump at Badminton, England, one of six classic events that include the Rolex Kentucky event in the United States and the Australian International Three Day Event in Adelaide.

Team chasing

This sport is essentially a team version of horse trials. Four competitors tackle the cross-country course as a team, and the team with the fastest overall time wins. Usually, one or more of the fences is a "dressing" fence that at least three of the four horses have to jump side-by-side.

Irish Draft

Originally bred as a lightweight draft horse with more power than the native Irish ponies, the Irish Draft has a complex ancestry involving Irish, English, Spanish, and Arabian breeds. Some Clydesdale genes were introduced in the late 19th century, but this was not a success and has been counteracted by infusions of Thoroughbred blood. The result is a versatile horse with a calm temperament that is excellent for competition, but also a prime choice for police work in stressful situations.

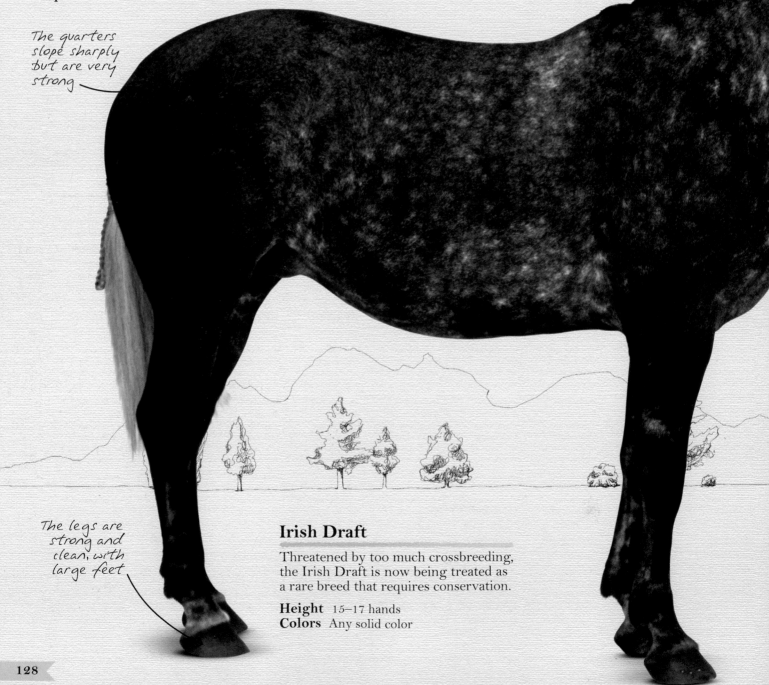

The quarters slope sharply but are very strong

The legs are strong and clean, with large feet

Irish Draft

Threatened by too much crossbreeding, the Irish Draft is now being treated as a rare breed that requires conservation.

Height 15–17 hands
Colors Any solid color

The neck is short, thick, and often slightly crested

A wide forehead gives the breed a look of intelligence

Trakehner

Developed in Prussia as a cavalry and carriage horse, this elegant warmblood is now a highly versatile competitor.

Height 16–16.2 hands
Colors Any solid color

High flier

Although this breed is a fine sport horse in its own right, Irish Draft mares are often crossed with Thoroughbred stallions to produce the Irish Sport Horse—a superb show jumper and eventer. Here the champion Irish Draft cross Carling King competes in the show jumping event of the 2004 Olympic Games in Athens, Greece.

Wielkopolski

This Polish breed is closely related to the Trakehner. It is an excellent jumper and eventer, and a stylish dressage mount.

Height 16–16.2 hands
Colors Any solid color

Endurance riding

For centuries, horses have been valued for their stamina as well as their speed. The ability to keep going hour after hour was vital for long-distance work such as cattle driving. But spending hours in the saddle is also a test for the rider, and in recent decades such endurance riding has become an organized sport, with horses and riders covering up to 100 miles (160 km) a day.

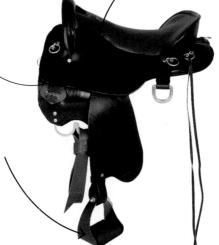

Comfortable padded seat

An endurance saddle must be light for the horse to carry

The stirrups have a wide tread to aid balance

High Sierra
Endurance riding became a formal sport in California in 1955, when a group of riders crossed the Sierra Nevada mountains from Lake Tahoe to Auburn in less than 24 hours. This 100 mile (160 km) ride is now known as the Tevis Cup, and is notorious for its rugged terrain and exhausting heat.

Lightweight saddle
Endurance saddles are designed to be light yet comfortable for horse and rider. Many competitors prefer lightweight designs based on Western saddles, such as this one. The horses may wear protective boots, but there are few rules and the choice of tack is up to the riders.

Stage by stage
Endurance rides are divided into stages with compulsory stops between each stage, and every rider has a route map showing the checkpoints and any natural obstacles. At each checkpoint, the horses are fed, watered, and inspected by a vet, and any horse considered unfit to continue is eliminated from the competition.

Winning form
In most events, the first horse to cross the finish line and still be "fit to continue" wins. But awards are also given for the best-conditioned horses that finish in the top ten. The prize for best-conditioned horse overall is often more valued than the winning prize.

Akhal-Teke

Bred to cope with the climatic extremes of the central Asian deserts, the Akhal-Teke is one of the oldest of all breeds, with a history dating back at least 1,000 years, and possibly much longer. Throughout that time, it has been purebred by the tribal people of Turkmenistan as both a warrior's charger and a racehorse. The harsh realities of tribal life in a hostile environment ensured that only the fittest survived, and as a result it has immense endurance and stamina, as well as the ability to reach high speeds.

The croup is sloping, and the tail set low

The body is slim and shallow

The legs are long and fine-boned with hard feet

Akhal-Teke

This breed is an athletic show jumper, but its real strength is in endurance events, where it has no equal.

Height 14.3–15.2 hands
Colors Dun, chestnut, bay, gray, black

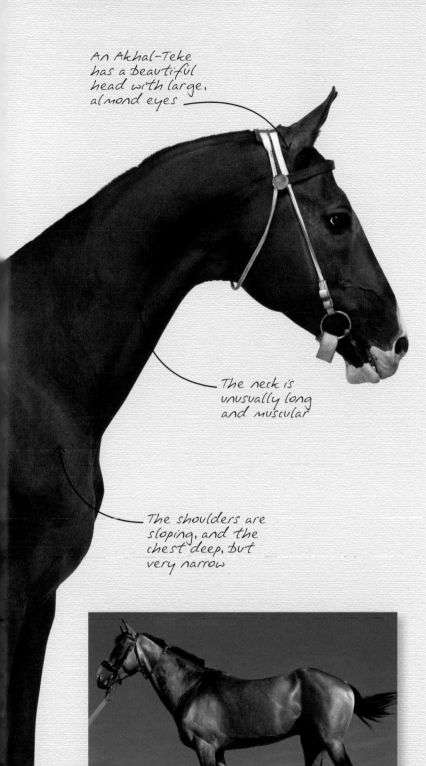

An Akhal-Teke has a beautiful head with large, almond eyes

The neck is unusually long and muscular

The shoulders are sloping, and the chest deep, but very narrow

Golden horses

Many Akhal-Tekes have a honey-colored coat, with black points and a gleaming golden sheen that is unique to the breed. This emphasizes their very lean, elegant form, which traditional breeders accentuate by making sure that the horses have no excess fat on their bodies.

Similar breeds

Kabardin

This rugged mountain horse from the northern Caucasus is very sure-footed and has great powers of endurance.

Height 14.2–15.2 hands
Colors Bay, brown, or black

Karabakh

Bred in Azerbaijan, this tough mountain horse has Kabardin and Akhal-Teke blood, and is often crossed with Arabs.

Height 14–15 hands
Colors Chestnut, bay, or dun

Bashkir Curly

Discovered living wild in Nevada in 1898, this curly-coated mountain horse is a very hardy but good-natured breed.

Height 14.2–15 hands
Colors Any color

Le Trec

Invented in France but now widely popular, Le Trec is a sport that tests the skills of map reading, navigation, and riding in open country. It is made up of three separate stages completed over one or two days: a mounted form of orienteering, a test of horse control, and an obstacle course event. Riders lose points through faults of various kinds, and the competitor who finishes with the most points is the winner.

Finding the way

In the orienteering stage, riders are given a set time to copy a route from a marked map onto their own map. They then follow this route by using the map and a compass. There are checkpoints along the way to make sure they get it right, and to control their speed. The riders must stop at the checkpoints, giving the horses a rest.

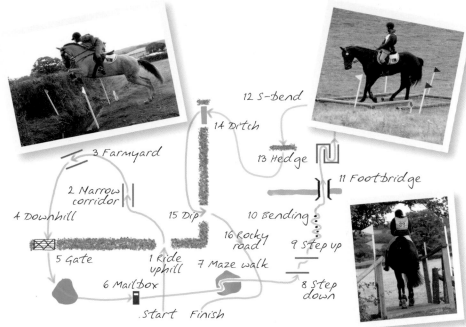

12 S-bend
14 Ditch
3 Farmyard
13 Hedge
11 Footbridge
2 Narrow corridor
15 Dip
10 Bending
4 Downhill
16 Rocky road
9 Step up
5 Gate
1 Ride uphill
7 Maze walk
8 Step down
6 Mailbox
Start   Finish

Staying in control

The second stage is designed to show that the riders have good control over their horses, first cantering, then walking. Each rider canters up a straight course in one direction, then walks back—but the canter has to be as slow as possible, and the walk as fast as possible.

Negotiating hazards

The obstacle course consists of up to 16 obstacles such as jumps, ditches, steps, narrow gates, and footbridges. There may even be obstacles that involve dismounting. All of these hazards have to be negotiated effectively in the correct order, within a set time, and with a certain style.

Hacking

Essentially, Le Trec is a competitive form of cross-country pleasure riding, or hacking—an activity that most riders enjoy. There is no serious element of competition involved in hacking, but it does demand the same skills—following a path, controlling your mount, and negotiating hazards.

More horseplay

In addition to racing their horses and pitting them against each other in jumping and endurance events, riders have found many other ways of using them for sports. These include various forms of hunting, team games such as polo, and mounted contests that were originally used as cavalry training exercises. Some of these sports have been played for centuries, but people invent new ones all the time.

Thrill of the chase

Riders have hunted on horseback for thousands of years. Their motives were partly practical, but they soon discovered that hunting involved an exhilarating cross-country chase. The same is true of drag hunts like this, where riders chase after hounds following an artificial scent trail.

Tent-pegging

Played in India since at least the 4th century BCE, this involves riding at a gallop and using a lance to pick up a small ground target. It is called tent-pegging because cavalry officers mounting a dawn raid on an enemy camp would use this technique to uproot tent pegs, making the tents collapse on their sleeping occupants.

Polo

This ball game probably originated as a battle-training exercise in Persia 2,500 years ago. A team of four tries to score goals against the other team using long-handled mallets. Fast and intense, each match is divided into six 7.5-minute chukkas to allow players to rest and change ponies.

Polocrosse

Devised in Australia in the 1930s, polocrosse is a mounted version of lacrosse. Three players on each team are armed with racquets, which they use to catch, carry, and throw the ball. One player is a striker, who tries to outflank his or her opponents and score goals. As in polo, the game is divided into short chukkas.

Barrel racing

The main women's rodeo event in America, barrel racing involves riding a clover-leaf course around three barrels arranged in a triangle. Competitors ride one at a time against the clock, each aiming for the quickest time without knocking any barrels over. This take nerve and a fast, athletic horse.

Kathiawari

This small horse gets its name from the Kathiawar Peninsula in Gujarat, western India, where it has been bred since the 14th century. Local pony stock was improved with a lot of Arabian blood to create a naturally tough, frugal breed with great stamina, endurance, and a touch of class. Highly regarded in its native region, where it was traditionally bred by wealthy local families, it is a preferred mount for the sport of tent-pegging. It is also used by the local Gujarat mounted police.

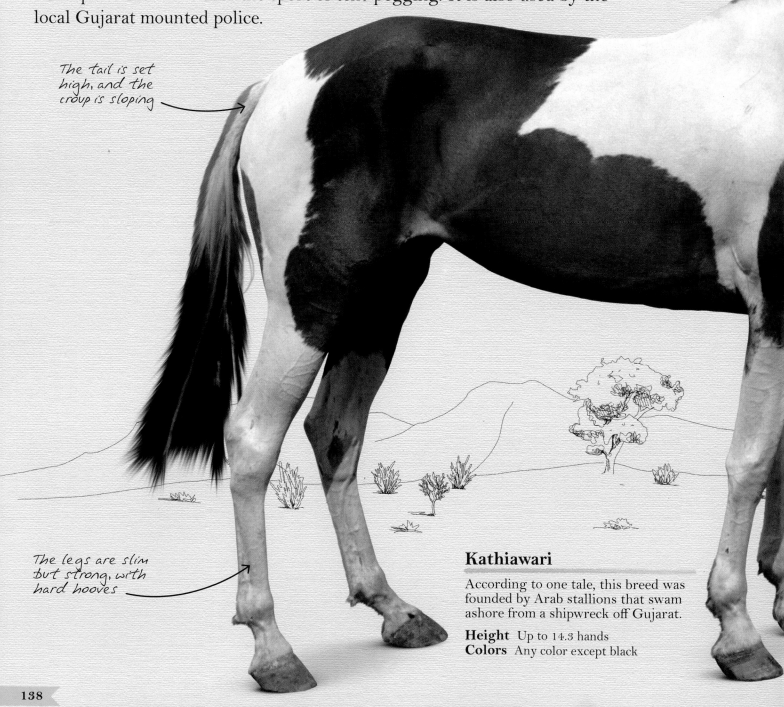

The tail is set high, and the croup is sloping

The legs are slim but strong, with hard hooves

Kathiawari

According to one tale, this breed was founded by Arab stallions that swam ashore from a shipwreck off Gujarat.

Height Up to 14.3 hands
Colors Any color except black

The neck is short, but graceful

Large, mobile ears curve together at the tips

The breed has a broad forehead and short muzzle

The chest is narrow but deep

Karabair

This ancient breed from Uzbekistan is a fusion of Mongol and Arab blood. It is often used in the local sport of buzkashi.

Height 14.2–15 hands
Colors Mostly gray, bay, or chestnut

Distinctive headgear

Originally bred as a desert warrior's mount, the Kathiawari is known for its ability to survive on minimal rations in extreme heat. But a more obvious feature is its distinctive ears, which curve in to touch at the tips. It seems that it was selectively bred for this trait in the past.

Polo pony

A type rather than a breed, the polo pony is bred for speed and agility. In Argentina, polo ponies are bred using Thoroughbred and Criollo blood.

Height Average 15.1 hands
Colours Any color

Knight riders

During the Middle Ages, rich aristocrats rode into battle wearing so much steel armor that they were virtually impregnable to attack by foot soldiers. However, one heavily armored knight could unhorse another using a long lance and his own considerable momentum. The defeated knight would be captured and held for ransom, which could be immensely profitable. The knights honed their skills by jousting with each other in competitions known as tournaments.

solid helmet with extravagant feathered plume

Royal patrons
Heavily armored cavalry became obsolete in the 14th century, but jousting survived as a sport for those wealthy enough to afford the elaborate armor required. English king Henry VIII was an enthusiast, as were many other European kings and nobles.

caparisons were embroidered with heraldic signs

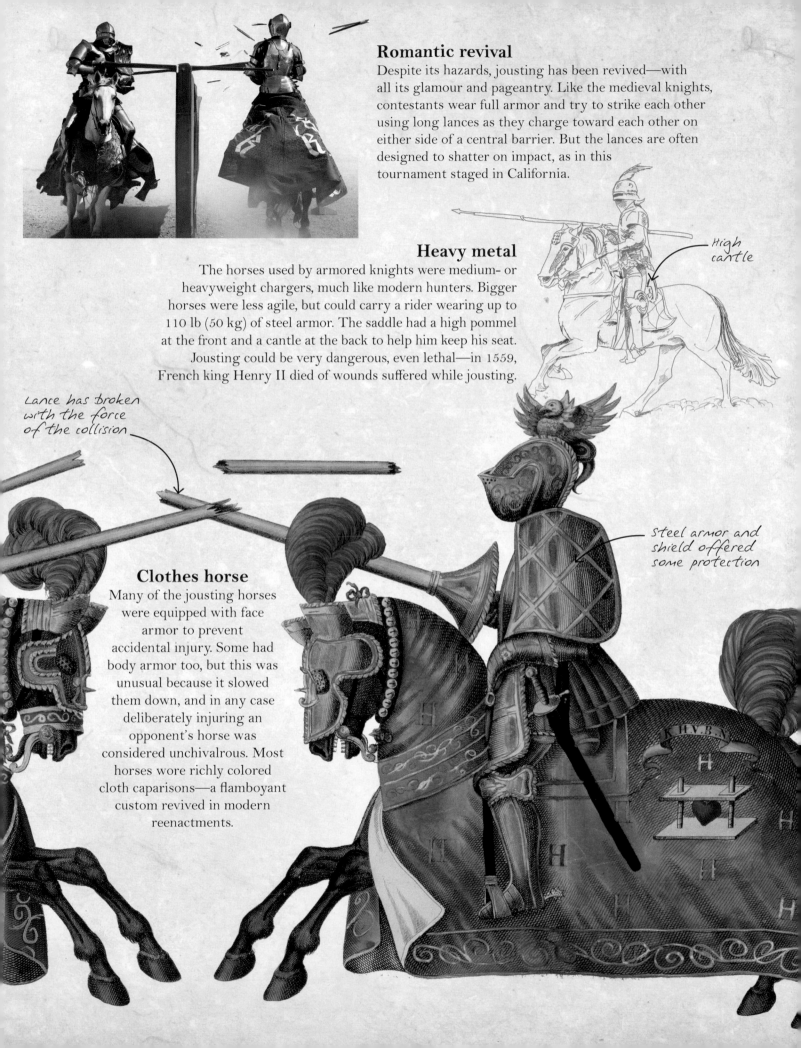

Romantic revival

Despite its hazards, jousting has been revived—with all its glamour and pageantry. Like the medieval knights, contestants wear full armor and try to strike each other using long lances as they charge toward each other on either side of a central barrier. But the lances are often designed to shatter on impact, as in this tournament staged in California.

High cantle

Heavy metal

The horses used by armored knights were medium- or heavyweight chargers, much like modern hunters. Bigger horses were less agile, but could carry a rider wearing up to 110 lb (50 kg) of steel armor. The saddle had a high pommel at the front and a cantle at the back to help him keep his seat. Jousting could be very dangerous, even lethal—in 1559, French king Henry II died of wounds suffered while jousting.

Lance has broken with the force of the collision

Steel armor and shield offered some protection

Clothes horse

Many of the jousting horses were equipped with face armor to prevent accidental injury. Some had body armor too, but this was unusual because it slowed them down, and in any case deliberately injuring an opponent's horse was considered unchivalrous. Most horses wore richly colored cloth caparisons—a flamboyant custom revived in modern reenactments.

Mounted games

Competitions designed for young riders often feature a variety of mounted games that test a range of riding skills. These events are known as gymkhanas, or omoksees in the Western United States. Organized by societies such as the Pony Club, they are mostly local contests that are open to complete beginners as well as more accomplished riders. But mounted games have also become part of major national competitions.

Bending poles

Skill and speed

Some mounted games are good tests of riding skill. In the pole bending race, for example, competitors zigzag between rows of poles like slalom skiers, trying to achieve the fastest time without knocking any down. Sometimes, two riders race each other instead of riding against the clock.

Fun for the young

Many mounted games are designed to entertain very young riders with activities such as popping balloons with a sharp stick, hooking "fish" with makeshift rods, or picking things out of a bucket. But they all demand some level of riding skill, and can inspire some surprisingly fierce competition.

Prince Philip Cup

In Britain, the Pony Club organizes gymkhana events that culminate in a mounted games final, where teams compete for the prestigious Prince Philip Cup at the national Horse of the Year Show. Despite its status, the event is designed for young riders of all abilities.

Vaulting

A very different style of mounted game has been refined into the sport of equestrian vaulting. The vaulters compete either individually or in teams, performing spectacular gymnastics on circling horses moving at a trot or canter. Some exercises are compulsory, but others are freestyle.

Keeping a pony

Owning a pony is a dream for many, and a dream come true for some. But a pony is a big responsibility. It needs to be checked several times a day, mucked out, fed, watered, and exercised. Anyone who has a pony knows that none of this is a chore—it is all part of the pleasure.

Stabling and feeding

A wild horse can go where it wants to find shelter, food, and water. A domestic pony, by contrast, is usually kept in a fenced paddock or a stable, so most of its needs have to be provided by its keeper. This is obvious if the pony is stabled, but the same is true even if it is kept on grass. Few paddocks are big enough to supply all a pony's needs, and grazing the same ground all the time can cause overgrazing and encourage internal parasites. The more ponies, the bigger the problem.

Warm and dry

A pony kept in a paddock needs a shelter from wind and rain. It doesn't have to be elaborate— a roofed, three-sided timber structure is fine—but it must be roomy, well drained, and easily accessible. The pony may also need a rug to protect it from cold weather, especially if its coat has been clipped.

poisonous plants such as ragwort should be pulled up

Green pastures

Ponies damage their paddocks by overgrazing, trampling, and avoiding distasteful plants so that they grow out of control. It is therefore important to reseed and fertilize the grass regularly. Any garbage that might harm the pony must be cleared away, and any droppings removed, because they may contain the eggs of intestinal parasites.

Clean and fit

A stabled pony needs bedding such as straw, shredded paper, or shavings. This must be kept clean by removing droppings several times a day and mucking out the soiled bedding daily. Most ponies also need at least four hours of exercise a day—either loose in a paddock or being ridden.

Food and water

Wild horses eat little and often, and a domestic pony needs to be fed on the same basis. If it has access to plenty of grass, it can help itself, but grass—or hay—is not enough for a pony that is ridden regularly. It also needs concentrated food, as well as access to a constant supply of fresh water.

Digestive system

A horse specializes in eating the most indigestible of foods—grass. It has an enlarged hindgut, which houses the colon, rectum, and cecum. Bacteria living in the cecum break down the tough plant fiber and turn it into sugar. But a horse has to eat a lot of food to get the nutrients it needs.

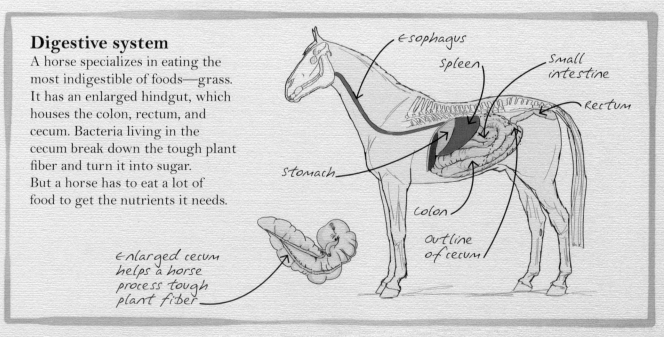

esophagus

spleen

small intestine

rectum

stomach

colon

outline of cecum

Enlarged cecum helps a horse process tough plant fiber

Grooming

Regular, thorough grooming will keep a pony clean, healthy, and looking good. It involves a lot more than simply brushing its coat, especially if preparing for a show, so it is important to be properly equipped. But the value of grooming goes well beyond appearances. It provides a daily opportunity to check a pony's health thoroughly, and it also helps create and strengthen the bond between a pony and its rider. But before a pony can be groomed, it may need to be caught, and this can sometimes be quite a challenge.

A soft-bristled body brush removes dirt and grease from the body, legs, mane, and tail

A damp water brush can be used to "lay" the mane and tail, so that the hairs stay in place for a show

How to catch a pony

Close the gate behind you and quietly approach the pony's shoulder with a head collar behind your back. Spend time petting the pony, then gently slip the lead rope over its neck, holding the rope as you work your way up to its face. Stroke the pony for a while before slipping on the head collar.

A pony's feet must be checked and cleaned out daily, using a hoof pick

Keeping clean

A pony's grooming needs vary according to how it is kept. A stabled horse must be groomed daily, while a grass-kept pony should not be brushed excessively, as this removes the essential oils from the coat that keep it dry. Basic grooming involves removing mud and sweat and cleaning the feet. A full groom is more effective when the pony is warm after exercise.

A metal curry comb is for cleaning brushes, and is never used on a pony

A mane comb is used for pulling the mane and separating hair for plaiting

A dandy brush (right) or a rubber curry comb can be used to remove thick, dried mud from the body

Two separate sponges should be kept: one to clean the eyes, nose, and muzzle, and one for the dock

A final polish with a damp grooming rag will remove any remaining dirt

Hoof oil helps keep the hooves in good condition, and looks good

After washing, excess water can be removed with a sweat scraper

Clipping

In winter, a horse grows a thicker coat. This is fine in the wild but not for a horse that is being worked hard, because it tends to overheat. Clipping the coat two or three times in winter helps prevent this. The clip is selective, leaving some areas untouched—such as the legs and saddle area in this hunter clip.

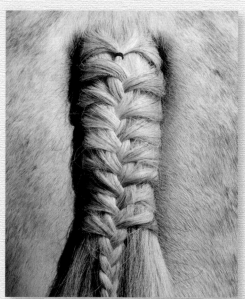

Showing a pony

If a pony is going to a show, it needs to look its best. Scissors can be used to trim the hair around the head and legs, and the mane can be "pulled" gently using a mane comb to pull out the longer hairs a few at a time. Some show classes also require the mane and tail to be plaited.

Horse and rider

Both a rider and a pony need the right equipment. This varies from pony to pony, and according to local tradition and the type of riding undertaken. Western riding, for example, is very different from European-style riding, and a dressage saddle is not suitable for a jumping event. But for hacking and non-competitive jumping, a general-purpose saddle and simple bridle are usually fine.

Riding clothes

The essentials for any riding activity are a body protector and a hard riding hat or helmet. Even the most experienced rider can have an accident. Proper riding boots are far safer than shoes, and stretchy jodhpurs are more comfortable than regular pants. A pair of gloves will protect hands.

A hard hat must be worn at all times

Long sleeves protect arms

Gloves help the rider grip the reins

Noseband

Cheekpiece

Breastplate can be used when jumping to prevent the saddle from sliding back

A girth holds the saddle in place

Staying safe

When on the street, a rider must be visible to drivers. A high-visibility yellow vest will be hard to miss, and similar fluorescent boots for the horse are excellent because their movement catches a driver's attention. A fluorescent rug over the pony's vulnerable rear end can also help.

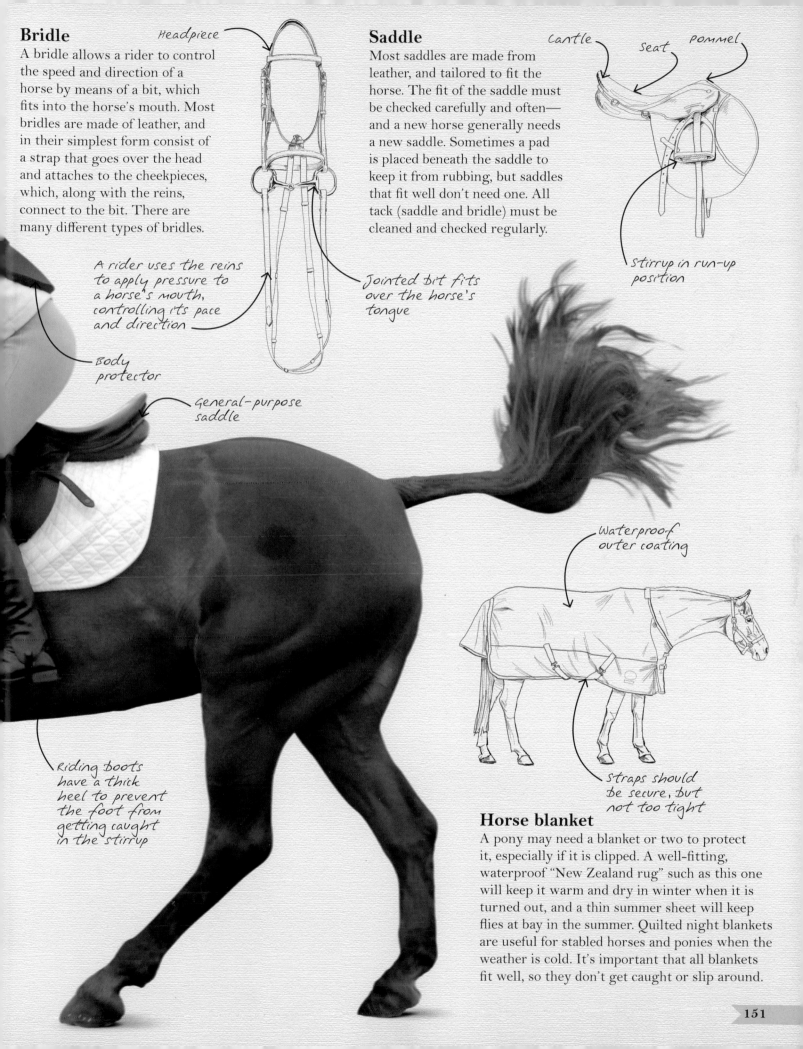

Bridle

A bridle allows a rider to control the speed and direction of a horse by means of a bit, which fits into the horse's mouth. Most bridles are made of leather, and in their simplest form consist of a strap that goes over the head and attaches to the cheekpieces, which, along with the reins, connect to the bit. There are many different types of bridles.

Headpiece

A rider uses the reins to apply pressure to a horse's mouth, controlling its pace and direction

Jointed bit fits over the horse's tongue

Body protector

General-purpose saddle

Riding boots have a thick heel to prevent the foot from getting caught in the stirrup

Saddle

Most saddles are made from leather, and tailored to fit the horse. The fit of the saddle must be checked carefully and often—and a new horse generally needs a new saddle. Sometimes a pad is placed beneath the saddle to keep it from rubbing, but saddles that fit well don't need one. All tack (saddle and bridle) must be cleaned and checked regularly.

Cantle

Seat

Pommel

Stirrup in run-up position

Waterproof outer coating

Straps should be secure, but not too tight

Horse blanket

A pony may need a blanket or two to protect it, especially if it is clipped. A well-fitting, waterproof "New Zealand rug" such as this one will keep it warm and dry in winter when it is turned out, and a thin summer sheet will keep flies at bay in the summer. Quilted night blankets are useful for stabled horses and ponies when the weather is cold. It's important that all blankets fit well, so they don't get caught or slip around.

Hoof and tooth care

A pony's hooves and teeth grow continuously, so they need regular attention. Its hooves in particular need to be checked frequently, because if there is any problem with them, the pony will go lame and will not be rideable. It will also need to be shoed by a professional farrier, so its hooves can cope with carrying a rider over hard surfaces such as roads. Since the farrier is an expert at spotting hoof problems, regular shoeing will reveal any foot trouble before it becomes serious.

On the hoof
The hoof is an enlarged toenail, which covers and protects the foot. A pony's weight is carried by the wall of the hoof, made of tough horn that grows continuously as the hoof wears down. The area within the hoof wall— the sole—is protected by a wedge of horn called the frog.

Foot check
Each hoof is protected by an iron shoe, so it does not wear down as it would in the wild. As the hoof grows, it changes the foot shape, putting pressure on the back of the foot that may cause collapsed heels. This means that a pony's feet need to be checked by a farrier every four to six weeks.

Iron shoes

Horseshoes are made by a blacksmith, using iron bars heated in a furnace and bent around an anvil with a hammer. Nail holes are then punched through the red-hot metal. Metal "clips" at the front or sides of a shoe prevent it from slipping. Shoes are made in various sizes, but final fitting is done when shoeing.

Blacksmith's hammer

pincers

Shoeing

The farrier carefully removes the old shoe with pincers, then trims and files the hoof (inset). He selects a shoe, heats it, and holds it against the hoof to make a burn mark that shows where any adjustments are needed. He reshapes the shoe, then nails it to the hoof with each nail slanting outward. He then bends the protruding nail tip down to secure it.

Teeth and age

The three pairs of incisor teeth at the front of a horse's mouth change their angle with age. This affects the way they wear down, creating differently shaped wear facets or "tables" on each tooth. With experience, you can tell exactly how old a horse is by checking the state of its teeth.

A young horse has upright teeth with oval wear facets or "tables."

5 years

At 12 years old, the teeth are sloping, and as a result their tables are rounded.

12 years

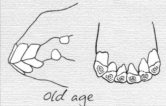

The teeth of an old horse slope so much that their tables are virtually triangular.

Old age

Checking teeth

A horse's teeth keep growing to make up for the wear caused by chewing tough, gritty grass, but they need to be checked regularly for uneven wear by a horse dentist or vet. Every six months or so, the teeth may need rasping to remove painful sharp edges, especially if a horse is stabled.

Looking good

A healthy pony should be bright-eyed with a smooth, glossy coat. Its skin should be relaxed and elastic, and it should stand on all four feet (or maybe with one hindfoot rested). It should be eating and drinking well, and passing normal droppings and urine.

Staying healthy

In addition to regularly having its feet and teeth checked, a pony needs to be watched for any other signs of poor health. Some, such as open wounds, are obvious and often easy to treat. But it is useful to keep an eye out for any hint that something else is wrong and to know when to ask for professional help. Some common problems can be prevented by vaccination and other types of medication, but many can also be avoided by good stable hygiene and pasture management.

When to get help

Even the slightest change in a pony's normal behavior could indicate a problem. Any loss of condition or strange behavior should be investigated, and this might involve calling the vet—especially if the pony is showing signs of real distress.

Minor wounds

Foreign objects should be removed, and firm pressure applied with a sterile pad to stop the bleeding. Hair should be trimmed and the wound cleaned with boiled, cooled water containing a little salt or antiseptic; a fresh piece of cotton wool should be used for each wipe. Finally, the area should be dried and wound powder or cream applied.

Inside view

It is useful to know how a horse is put together. Its legs are very long for speed, and its spine relatively stiff—which is why a person can ride a horse without injuring

Worming

Intestinal parasites can be kept in check by removing droppings from a pony's paddock and, ideally, grazing other animals on the pasture. But parasites also need to be controlled by regular worming at six-to-eight-week intervals. Different worms are treated with different medication—a vet can advise.

Vaccinations

A local vet will know which vaccinations a pony needs. These will protect it from equine diseases such as herpes, influenza, strangles, and tetanus. Some of the vaccinations are essential for any pony, but others may not be needed if the disease is rare in the area.

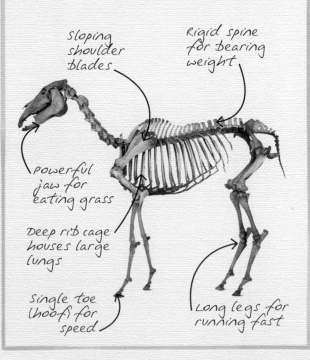

Sloping shoulder blades

Rigid spine for bearing weight

Powerful jaw for eating grass

Deep rib cage houses large lungs

Single toe (hoof) for speed

Long legs for running fast

Glossary

Bay
A horse coat color, basically reddish brown but varying, with black points (mane, tail, and lower legs).

Binocular vision
Seeing the same view with two eyes at once, giving a perception of distance and depth.

Bloodline
The ancestry of a horse, in terms of inherited blood.

Boots
Fabric or leather sheaths that strap around a horse's lower legs, usually for protection from injury.

Browse
To eat leaves, rather than grass.

Cantle
A raised, curved section at the back of a saddle.

Coachwork
The main body of a coach.

Coldblood
A type of horse with a placid nature; usually a working breed such as a Shire.

Combination fence
A fence in a jumping competition with two or more sections that the horse must jump in quick succession.

Condition
State of fitness and health.

Conformation
A horse's basic form, defined mainly by its skeleton.

Convex profile
A face with a shape that bulges outward; also called a Roman nose.

Croup
The top part of a horse's hindquarters.

Dished profile
A face with a slightly hollow (concave) shape; the opposite of a convex profile.

Dorsal stripe
A dark stripe extending down a horse's back.

Draft horse
A horse used for hauling a wagon, carriage, or other vehicle.

Dressage
A competition that tests training, obedience, and precision.

Dun
A horse coat color, consisting of yellow hair growing from black skin, usually with black points (mane, tail, and lower legs).

Equestrian
A rider, or an event involving horses and riders.

Equine
Relating to horses (family Equidae).

Eventing
Taking part in riding competitions that combine show jumping, dressage, and a cross-country phase.

Farrier
A specialist in shoeing horses and correcting hoof problems.

Feather
Long hair around a horse's foot.

Feral horse
A horse that lives wild, but either was domestic or is descended from domestic stock.

Gait
The sequence in which a horse moves its legs at various speeds.

Gelding
A male horse that has been neutered.

Genus
A scientific classification of a group of living things, and the first part of the scientific name of any organism. All horses belong to the genus *Equus*.

Gray
A coat color. The skin is black but the hairs are mostly white.

Hacking
Pleasure riding.

Hames
The two metal frames attached to each side of a horse collar, with hooks for the chains used for haulage.

Hands
The system used to measure the height of a horse; one "hand" is approximately the width of an adult man's hand, but is defined as four inches (10 cm).

Harness
The equipment that enables a horse to pull a heavy load.

Harness racing
Racing using single horses harnessed to light two-wheeled buggies, or sulkies. The horses may either trot or pace, depending on the race rules.

Hotblood
A typically temperamental horse such as an Arab or Thoroughbred, bred for racing and similar high-performance sports.

Hybrid
A cross between two species, for example a mule (a donkey-horse cross). Most hybrids, including mules, are sterile and cannot breed.

Lateral gait
A type of movement in which the horse moves both legs on the same side at the same time.

Mare
A mature female horse.

Mealy
An oatmeal color, typically on a horse's muzzle.

Mule
An artificial donkey-horse cross in which the father was a donkey and the mother was a horse. The reverse is called a hinny, but is much rarer.

Mustang
An American wild horse descended from domestic stock, and therefore technically a feral horse.

Pacing
A fast lateral gait, roughly equivalent to trotting.

Packhorse
A horse used to carry a load on its back. Ponies and mules are used in the same way.

Pampas
Natural temperate grasslands in South America; the equivalent of prairies.

Parasite
A living thing that lives on or in another living thing, and gets its food from it.

Pommel
A raised, solid section at the front of a saddle.

Predator
An animal that kills and eats other animals.

Primeval
A primitive form of something.

Quarters
The hips of a horse.

Ranch
A type of farm in which all the land is used as pasture for raising grazing animals such as cattle or horses.

Roan
A chestnut (strawberry roan), bay (red roan), or black (blue roan) coat interspersed with white hairs.

Rodeo
A sports event centered around the Western riding skills developed by cowboys in the American West.

Rosette
A colorful badge with ribbons presented as a prize and usually worn on a horse's bridle.

Rug
For a horse, a protective cover for the body; another name for a blanket. A New Zealand rug is worn outside in winter.

Sire
To be the father. A male horse might sire several foals.

Species
A scientific classification of a particular living thing, and the second part of its scientific name. The plains zebra belongs to the genus *Equus*, but its species is *quagga* so its full scientific name is *Equus quagga*.

Square gait
A way of moving in which the horse moves each foot in turn in an even, four-beat sequence. The most common square gait is the walk.

Stallion
A male horse, more than four years old, that has not been neutered and is therefore able to breed.

Stamina
The ability to remain active over a long period of time without tiring.

Steppe
Natural temperate grasslands in Asia; the equivalent of prairies.

Studbook
The book used by a breed society to record the pedigrees of purebred stock.

Sulky
A very light two-wheeled buggy used for racing; sometimes known as a "bike" because it often has bicycle wheels.

Tack
A general term for saddles, bridles, and other saddlery equipment.

Warmblood
A type of horse that combines placid coldblood ancestry and high-spirited hotblood ancestry, and ideally is both good-tempered and athletic.

Western riding
The riding style developed in the American West, derived from the Spanish traditions used in Mexico.

Withers
The highest part of a horse's back, between the shoulders. A horse's height is measured at the withers.

Index

Acknowledgments

DK would like to thank:
John Searcy for Americanization, Jenny Sich for proofreading, Jackie Brind for preparing the index, Stefan Podhorodecki for additional design, Rose Horridge and Romaine Werblow for additional picture research, Francesca Wardell for additional pre-production work, and Steve Willis for color correction work.

Note on the story of Mancha and Gato (pages 72–73): The Long Riders' Guild is an association of men, women, and children from 44 countries who have made an equestrian journey of 1,000 miles or more. The youngest Long Rider was three years old when she qualified! Long Riders have explored every continent, including Antarctica. Aimé Tschiffely is the most famous and the Long Riders' Guild publishes the story of his journey, *A Tale of Two Horses.*
www.thelongridersguild.com / www.aimetschiffely.org

The publisher would like to thank the following for their kind permission to reproduce their photographs:

(Key: a—above; b—below/bottom; c—center; f—far; l—left; r—right; t—top)

2-3 SuperStock: Belinda Images. **4 Dorling Kindersley:** Judith Miller / Ken Grant (br); University Museum of Archaeology and Anthropology, Cambridge (bl). **6-7 Corbis:** Tetra Images. **8 Alamy Images:** blickwinkel / Hecker (cra). **Corbis:** Jeff Vanuga (bl). **Dorling Kindersley:** Natural History Museum, London (tr). **9 Alamy Images:** Peter Llewellyn (tr). **Corbis:** Ocean (bl); Konrad Wothe / Minden Pictures (cl). **Getty Images:** Jonathan and Angela (br). **SuperStock:** Minden Pictures (cr). **10 Dorling Kindersley:** University Museum of Archaeology and Anthropology, Cambridge (tr). **FLPA:** Yva Momatiuk & John Eastcott / Minden Pictures (cr). **10-11 Science Photo Library:** Pascal Goetgheluck (b). **11 Corbis:** Alberto Aja / EPA (cr). **Science Photo Library:** Tom McHugh (tl). **12 FLPA:** Terry Whittaker (cl). **SuperStock:** NaturePL (bl). **12-13 Corbis:** Ocean (c). **13 Corbis:** Arctic-Images (tr); Peter Johnson (crb). **15 Corbis:** Frans Lanting (b). **Klaus Rudloff:** (br). **16-17 Alamy Images:** Jürgen Schulzki (b). **16 SuperStock:** Photononstop (tr). **17 akg-images:** Erich Lessing (tl). **Getty Images:** G. Nimatallah / De Agostini (tr). **SuperStock:** De Agostini (crb). **18 Alamy Images:** Wildlife GmbH (bl). **24 Alamy Images:** gezmen (b). **Corbis:** (tl). **Getty Images:** Alexander Nemenov / AFP (tr). **22 Corbis:** Frank Lukasseck (bl). **24 Corbis:** The Gallery Collection (bl). **24-25 The Art Archive:** De Agostini Picture Library / M. Seemuller (c). **25 Corbis:** Dean Conger (tr); Said Hijran Frogh / Demotix (crb). **27 Bob Langrish:** . **28-29 Corbis:** Arctic-Images. **30 Alamy Images:** Shaun McCaughan (clb). **Getty Images:** Art Wolfe / The Image Bank (tr). **Soundview Shetlands:** (br). **31 Alamy Images:** Juniors Bildarchiv / F368 (tc); Wildlife GmbH (main image). **Corbis:** Kit Houghton (tl). **Fotolia:** Zoe (tr). **32 Alamy Images:** David Bagnall (bl). **33 Dorling Kindersley:** Courtesy of Allensdale Vampire and Owner, Miss H. Houlden (tr); Courtesy of Mrs Rae Turner, Bowerwood Stud, Hampshire (br). **34 Corbis:** Yann Arthus-Bertrand / Leemage / Universal Images Group (cl). **35 akg-images:** R. u. S. Michaud (b). **Corbis:** Werner Forman Archive (main image). **© Dark Horse Records trademark is owned by Umlaut Corporation:** (tl). **36 Corbis:** Morteza Nikoubazl / Reuters (bl). **37 fotoLibra :** Andrew Lawrence (tr).

38 Corbis: Craig Lovell (ca). **Dreamstime.com:** Jinfeng Zhang (clb). **Getty Images:** Tim Graham (crb). **39 Alamy Images:** Blickwinkel / Lenz (main image). **SuperStock:** NaturePL (bl). **40 Corbis:** Destinations (bl). **42 Alamy Images:** Carol Dixon (bl); Wayne Hutchinson (tr). **42-43 Alamy Images:** Wayne Hutchinson (c). **43 Alamy Images:** Les Gibbon (crb); Wayne Hutchinson (tc). **Danni Showers (via Flickr):** (tr). **44-45 Dreamstime.com:** Isselee (c). **44 Corbis:** Gérard Labriet / Photononstop (tl). **46 Alamy Images:** Juniors Bildarchiv / F381 (crb). **Corbis:** (clb). **Dreamstime.com:** Susinder (tr). **Getty Images:** Tim Graham (br). **47 Corbis:** Lothar Lenz. **49 Alamy Images:** Joachim Hiltmann / imagebroker (tr). **50 Getty Images:** Paul Trummer / The Image Bank (bl). **52 Alamy Images:** Geraint Lewis (bl). **Wikipedia:** (tl). **52-53 Alamy Images:** Mary Evans Picture Library (main image). **53 Alamy Images:** AF archive (cra); Moviestore collection Ltd (tl). **55 Alamy Images:** Manfred Grebler (tr). **56-57 Getty Images:** Cynthia Baldauf. **58 Alamy Images:** RIA Novosti (clb). **Getty Images:** Philippe Henry / First Light (cl). **58-59 Alamy Images:** South West Images Scotland (c). **59 Corbis:** Patrick Pleul / DPA (tr). **Dorling Kindersley:** Judith Miller / Ken Grant (t). **Getty Images:** Fox Photos / Hulton Archive (crb). **60 Alamy Images:** M. Delpho / Arco Images (bl). **61 Dorling Kindersley:** Courtesy of Kentucky Horse Park, USA (tr). **62 Alamy Images:** Johan De Meester / Arterra Picture Library (cla). **Corbis:** Bertrand Gardel / Hemis (cra). **62-63 Getty Images:** Lake County Museum / Curt Teich Postcard Archives. **63 Science Photo Library:** Sheila Terry (cra). **SuperStock:** Science and Society (tl). **64 Alamy Images:** Derek Middleton / FLPA (bl). **66 Corbis:** Blue Jean Images (tr). **66-67 Corbis:** Philip Spruyt / Stapleton Collection (Egyptian scene). **67 Alamy Images:** Pictorial Press Ltd (cla). **Getty Images:** G. Dagli Orti / De Agostini (tr). **68 Corbis:** Carson Ganci / Design Pics (tl); Dale C. Spartas (clb). **Getty Images:** Joel Sartore / National Geographic (cla). **68-69 Corbis:** Frank Lukasseck (main image). **69 Alamy Images:** Christopher Pillitz (crb). **Corbis:** (tr). **72 The Long Rider's Guild (www.thelongridersguild.com / www.aimetschiffely.org)** (clb). **73 Alamy Images:** Richard Slater. **Corbis:** Kit Houghton (tr). **74-75 Corbis:** Eddie Keogh / X01801 / Reuters. **76 Kit Houghton / Houghton's Horses:** **77 Alamy Images:** Blickwinkel / Lenz (crb). **Bob Langrish:** (bl). **78 Corbis:** José Fuste Raga (bl). **79 Alamy Images:** Juniors Bildarchiv / F315 (br). **80 Corbis:** Lothar Lenz (tc/star). **Getty Images:** Nancy Nehring / Photodisc (tr). **81 Alamy Images:** Manfred Grebler (tc); Pat Kerrigan (tr); Kim Kaminski (cra). **Corbis:** Bernard Bisson / Sygma (bc); Ken Gillespie / All Canada Photos (tl). **82 Alamy Images:** Jürgen Schulzki (bl). **84 The Bridgeman Art Library:** Museo Nacional de Historia de Chapultepec, Mexico / photo: Michel Zabe / AZA INBA (tl). **Getty Images:** Science & Society Picture Library (bc). **85 Corbis:** PoodlesRock (b). **Bob Langrish:** (tr). **86 DLILLC** (clb). **Getty Images:** Michel Cavalier / Hemis.fr (crb). **87 Alamy Images:** Nigel Pavitt / John Warburton-Lee Photography (tl). **Corbis:** Arctic-Images (crb). **Getty Images:** Jeff Foott / Discovery Channel Images (clb). **88 Corbis:** Kit Houghton (bl). **90-91 Getty Images:** Chris Ison / AFP (main image). **90 Alamy Images:** Rex Moreton / Bubbles Photolibrary (br). **91 Alamy Images:** Gianni Dagli Orti / The Art Archive (crb). **Getty Images:** Science & Society Picture Library (bl). **93 Dorling Kindersley:** Courtesy of Darwin Olsen, Kentucky Horse Park, USA (tr). **Kit Houghton / Houghton's Horses:** (tl). **94 Corbis:** Bettmann (tr/stamps). **95 TopFoto.co.uk:** The Granger Collection (bc). **Wikipedia:** (bl). **96 Alamy Images:** Interfoto (crb). **Corbis:** (l). **97 akg-images:** Interfoto (fcrb). **Corbis:** Fine Art Photographic Library (t); Steven Vidler /

Eurasia Press (bl). **Dorling Kindersley:** The Board of Trustees of the Royal Armouries (crb/sword). **99 Corbis:** Kit Houghton (clb). **100 Corbis:** Dominic Ebenbichler / Reuters (tr); Herwig Prammer / Reuters (cra); Eddie Keogh / Reuters (crb). **Getty Images:** G. Nimatallah / De Agostini (cl). **Lebrecht Music and Arts:** leemage (bc). **101 Corbis:** Pascal Deloche / Sygma (main image). **IPC+ Syndication:** Horse and Hound (bc). **102 Alamy Images:** Blickwinkel / Lenz (bl). **104-105 SuperStock:** Juniors. **106 The Bridgeman Art Library:** Yale Center for British Art, Paul Mellon Collection, USA (br). **Getty Images:** Ronald Martinez (clb). **106-107 Corbis:** Leo Mason (main image). **106-107 Alamy Images:** Apex News and Pictures Agency (bc). **Press Association Images:** Graham Stuart / PA Archive (bl). **109 Alamy Images:** M&N (crb). **Corbis:** Bettmann (tr). **110 Corbis:** William Manning (clb). **112 Getty Images:** Silver Screen Collection (bl). **112-113 Corbis:** Andrew Cooper / Columbia / Spyglass / Bureau L.A. Collection (c). **113 Alamy Images:** AF archive (bl). **Corbis:** Bureau L.A. Collection / Sygma (cra). **114-115 Corbis:** Leo Mason (main image). **115 Alamy Images:** Michelle Gilders Canada West (bc); Paul Mogford (c). **Corbis:** Tony Kurdzuk / Star Ledger (t). **116-117 Dorling Kindersley:** Courtesy of Farrington Stables and Estate of Paul Siebert, Kentucky Horse Park, USA (main image). **117 Corbis:** Tim Clayton (tr). **118-119 Corbis:** Redlink (main image). **119 Getty Images:** Christof Koepsel / Bongarts (clb); Jochen Luebke / AFP (crb). **IPC+ Syndication:** Horse and Hound (tl/gloves). **SBM Photographic:** (cra). **121 Corbis:** Larry W. Smith / EPA (bl). **122 Corbis:** Leo Mason (bc). **Getty Images:** Mauricio Lima / AFP (cl). **122-123 Getty Images:** Al Bello (c). **123 Corbis:** Michael St Maur Sheil (br). **125 Corbis:** Sampics (clb). **126 Alamy Images:** Equine Photos (tr). **Bob Langrish:** (fclb). **127 Bob Langrish:** (r). **PC Images:** (bl). **129 Getty Images:** Robert Laberge (clb). **130 Hughes Photography - Melinda Hughes. 131 ©2011 FFG Photography By Darin Pointer:** (crb). **HorseSaddleShop.com:** (cra). **Bob Langrish:** (clb). **133 Corbis:** Reza / Webistan (clb). **134-135 Kit Houghton / Houghton's Horses:** (b). **134 Mike Nichols:** (tr). **135 Kit Houghton / Houghton's Horses:** (tl, tc, ftr, fcra). **136 Alamy Images:** Farlap (cl). **Farrukh Pitafi:** (bc). **137 Alamy Images:** Nico Smit (tr). **Corbis:** Tim Clayton (main image); Matt Cohen / ZUMA Press (crb). **139 Corbis:** (clb). **140 Getty Images:** Leemage / Universal Images Group (clb). **140-141 The Bridgeman Art Library:** Private Collection / The Stapleton Collection (b/main image). **141 Corbis:** Brian Cahn (tl). **142 Alamy Images:** Mark Richardson (cr). **Tom James:** (c). **Bob Langrish:** (clb, br). **Press Association Images:** Steve Parsons / PA Archive (tr). **143 Getty Images:** Jean-François Monier / AFP (b); Matthew Lewis (main image). **144-145 SuperStock:** Juniors. **146 Alamy Images:** Peter Titmuss (crb); Kathy Wright (clb). **Bob Langrish:** (tr). **147 Alamy Images:** The Photolibrary Wales (t). **148 Kit Houghton / Houghton's Horses:** (clb, bl). **149 Getty Images:** Martin Child / Photographer's Choice RF (crb). **150 Alamy Images:** Jeff Morgan 13 (clb). **152 Alamy Images:** Joe Blossom (clb). **Corbis:** David Harrigan / ableimages (bl). **152-153 Alamy Images:** Garry Bowden (c). **153 Alamy Images:** Tim Duckworth (bc); Mike Rex (tl). **Dreamstime.com:** Oleksii Sergieiev (cra); Svlumagraphica (tr). **154 Corbis:** Paul A. Souders. **155 Alamy Images:** Angela Hampton Picture Library (tr); Mikhail Kondrashov "fotomik" (bl). **Dorling Kindersley:** Natural History Museum, London (br). **Bob Langrish:** (cla, clb).

All other images © Dorling Kindersley
For further information see: www.dkimages.com